A Fountain:
The Best of the Water Books

David K. Reynolds, Ph.D.

Dedication

For my teachers, my colleagues, my students, and my family—
Reality's representatives.

Acknowledgments

My work is supported, in part, by grants from the Mental Health Okamoto Memorial Foundation. My teachers and students in Japan and North America continue to offer me lessons. Some of those lessons I notice and incorporate into Constructive Living. Unfortunately, too much of their teaching goes unnoticed. My thanks to Jim Guswiler for pulling together his favorite quotes from the Water Books, edited and listed in the final chapter.

Contents

I. What is Constructive Living?
Why Water? (from A Thousand Waves)

II. Constructive Living and Feelings

III. Constructive Living and the Mind

On General Principles (from Pools of Lodging for the Moon)
Blind Spots (from Pools of Lodging for the Moon)
The Appeal of Pessimism (from Rainbow Rising from a Stream)
I Alone Suffer (from Rainbow Rising from a Stream)
Facts of Life (from Thirsty, Swimming in the Lake)
On Alcohol and Other Drugs (from Rainbow Rising from a Stream)
Realism (from Water Bears no Scars)

VII. Constructive Living Reflection
Misalignments (from Pools of Lodging for the Moon)
Warming Trend (from Even in Summer the Ice Doesn't Melt)
On Realistic Gratitude (from Pools of Lodging for the Moon)
The Perfect Mate (from Rainbow Rising from a Stream)
My Constructive Living reciprocity Reflections at 35,000 Feet (from Thirsty, Swimming in the Lake)

VIII. Constructive Living Maxims
Rain Maxims (from Rainbow Rising from a Stream
Swimming Maxims (from Thirsty, Swimming in the Lake)

IX. Constructive Living Koans
Rain Koans (from Rainbow Rising from a Stream)

X. Constructive Living Tales
Diamond Misery (from A Thousand Waves)
Runaway (from A Thousand Waves)
Being Ordinary (from A Thousand Waves)

X. Constructive Living Exercises

Exercises Amid the Waves (from A Thousand Waves) Exercises in the Rain (from Rainbow Rising from a Stream)
No Small Matter (from Pools of Lodging for the Moon)

XI. Constructive Living Quotes from the Water Books

INTRODUCTION

In the 1980's and 1990's a series of books about Constructive Living (CL) was published to introduce some fundamentally human ideas from Japan to an English-speaking readership. The titles of those books (for which I hold the copyrights) were:

Playing Ball on Running Water, Morrow, N.Y., 1984.
Even in Summer the Ice Doesn't Melt. Morrow, N.Y., 1986.
Water Bears No Scars, Morrow, N.Y., 1987.
Pools of Lodging for the Moon, Morrow, N.Y., 1989.
A Thousand Waves, Morrow, N.Y., 1990.
Thirsty, Swimming in the Lake, Morrow, N.Y., 1991.
Rainbow Rising from a Stream, Morrow, N.Y., 1992.

I call them the "Water Books." Each of the books had some form of water in the title. The titles were borrowed and adapted from various Chinese and Japanese sources. Water is both ordinary and vital to our existence. A more detailed explanation of the water theme is offered in the chapter "Why Water?" below.

The Water Books were an early and important part of the growing literature on Constructive Living in the West. Recently translated into Japanese volumes from the Water Books series have sparked renewed interest within the very country from which they emerged. They represent the beginning repayment of a forty year debt I owe my Japanese teachers of Morita Therapy and Constructive Living reciprocity Therapy. For many years now I have spent about six months of each year in Japan lecturing to Japanese in Japanese about these Japanese ideas.

There are now more than 200 trained and certified Constructive Living instructors around the world--in the United States, Canada, Japan, Mexico, New Zealand, England, Germany, the Philippines, Poland, and South Africa. Certification training currently takes place in the U.S., Canada, and Japan. Constructive Living books have been published in the U.S., England, Australia, Japan, China, and Germany. Well over 100,000 copies have been sold. It has taken twenty-five years to grow to this level of acceptance for a couple of reasons. The first has to do with quality control. Fewer than half the people who complete Constructive Living certification training are actually certified; the standards are that high.

The second reason for the measured growth of Constructive Living has to do with the difficulty of this lifestyle even for those who don't intend to become Constructive Living instructors. If Constructive Living promised the world freedom from neurotic misery, constant contentment and joy, spiritual highs, and an easy set of life principles it would be relatively easy to attract larger numbers of people. Instead Constructive

Living offers a realistic means of handling life suffering and joy, a way to find meaning in everyday life, and a challenging perspective on what it is to be "ordinary." The most effective way to determine the effectiveness of Constructive Living is to give it a tentative try. In this book you will find not only ideas to arouse your thinking, but also exercises to put these ideas into practice. Although I was introduced to the main themes of Constructive Living in Japan, I now see that they are basically human themes that have appeared in Judaism, Christianity, Sufism, Taoism and other religious and secular systems of thought and action. My job has been to make the principles understandable to Westerners and, as Japan becomes more Westernized, to the modern Japanese themselves.

I have selected some of my favorite chapters from the Water Books, edited them to bring them up to date, and organized them into groups on the basis of their primary content. Thank you for joining me for these moments as you read The Fountain: The Best of the Water Books.

I. WHAT IS CONSTRUCTIVE LIVING?

Why Water?

Natural qualities of water

Water is a symbol of the natural. By just naturally doing its thing, by just going about its water business in a water-like way, it accomplishes all sorts of feats. Not the least of its accomplishments is its ability to provide us with analogies that help make sense of human psychology and provide advice for successful living.

Most of my recent books have water in the title: *Playing Ball on Running Water;Even in Summer the Ice Doesn't Melt; Water Bears No Scars; Pools of Lodging for the Moon; A Thousand Waves; Rainbow Rising from a Stream; Flowing Bridges, Quiet Waters;* and *Plunging Through the Clouds* among others. In order, they refer, in part, to action in ever-changing time, the chill stiffness of neurosis, the purposeful now-centeredness of water, the ability of the moon to find a resting place in a hundred bowls of water without making reservations or receiving invitations, the splash an emotion makes on our thinking, hope arising from wisdom, stepping forward within uncertainty, and the subjective nature of situational changes.

The Eastern approaches to mental health which form what we call in the West "Constructive Living" are Morita therapy and

Constructive Living reciprocity therapy. They aim at helping us be natural. Some people believe that modern technology and other aspects of modern life have alienated us from Nature. What does it mean to become natural again?

Let's begin with a look at how water is natural. First, water accepts the reality of the situation it is in. It doesn't say "Now I'm in a glass, but I want to be in the ocean, so I'll sulk and daydream and not act like proper water." Only people do that. Water reflects whatever reality brings it.

"Tozan came to see Zen master Zenne of Kassan, and asked:
"'How are things?'
"'Just as they are.'" (Shibayama, 1970, p. 206)

In warm times water becomes warm, in cold times it becomes cold. It doesn't say, "I wish I were cool today. I shouldn't get this hot." It doesn't pretend it is warm when it is really cold. It simply accepts the reality of its temperature and goes about flowing toward the lowest place around.

People deny reality. They fight against real feelings caused by real circumstances. They build mental worlds of shoulds, oughts, and might-have-beens. Real changes begin with real appraisal and acceptance of what is. Then realistic action is possible.

Water flows around obstacles. It doesn't stop on its way down a riverbed to try to fight with the big rocks that oppose it. It just heads toward its goal and eventually wears down its opposition. Whether the obstacles wear down quickly or not, water manages to get where it aims to go without any long-term distraction. People tend to get distracted by feelings (for example, by anxiety before college exams) and shift away from their original purposes (for example, by trying to resolve the anxiety instead of continuing to study for the exams).

Water is wonderfully flexible. It fills the circumstances it is in. It takes the natural amount of time to get where it is going. It moves at a natural pace--now rushing quickly, now flowing slowly, depending on the circumstances. Some people seem to be rushing around all the time, trying to force time to fit their desires. Other people never seem to stir themselves to fast action.

What is so outstanding about these qualities? They are just the ordinary qualities of water. This chapter is about being ordinary and natural human beings in much the same way, and about the trouble we get ourselves into when we aren't realistic in the sense that water is realistic.

Constructive Living

Constructive Living is a bringing together of two psychotherapies and their associated lifeways with origins in Japan. As noted above, the two systems for dealing with human suffering and human existence are usually called Morita therapy and Constructive Living reciprocity therapy. Both were developed in this century, but their roots extend back for hundreds of years into the history of East Asia. Masatake Morita was a professor of psychiatry at Jikei University School of Medicine in Tokyo. Ishin Yoshimoto was a successful businessman who retired to become a lay priest in Nara. Morita's method has its origins in Zen Buddhist psychology (not Zen Buddhist religion), and Yoshimoto's Constructive Living reciprocity has its origins in Jodo Shinshu Buddhist psychology. Neither of these systems requires that one believe in Buddhism or have faith in anything other than one's own experience. They work as well for Christians and Moslems and Jews as for Buddhists. Both are built on the naturalistic observations of humans and on careful introspection by their founders. I think that as you read about Constructive Living you will be thinking that it isn't so very mystical and Oriental, but rather practical and human and, well, "realistic."

Morita therapy

Let us begin our consideration of Morita's ideas with the topic of feelings. Feelings are an important part of human life. There are feelings we like (feelings like confidence and love and happiness and satisfaction) and feelings we don't like (like loneliness and depression and fear and timidity). It isn't surprising that we try to generate some feelings and eliminate others. The problem with feelings, however, is that we cannot control them directly by our wills. We cannot sit down and concentrate and make our shyness go away or make ourselves stop feeling lonely on a Saturday night or make ourselves fall in love or out of love with someone. It just cannot be done. We cannot make ourselves stop feeling nervous before an exam, or anxious before asking someone out on a date, or tense before a job interview. Feelings are natural consequences of who we are and the situations we are in just like clouds are natural consequences of temperatures and pressures and humidity and so forth. Feelings are natural, and, naturally, they are just as uncontrollable as the weather.

Now, no one tries to fight with rain or fog. You never see anyone going outside waving a sword or a karate blow at rain clouds. And no ordinary humans try by their wills to make fog go away. No one ignores the weather, but we have all learned to dim our headlights in the fog, stay inside during hurricanes, and so forth. And we do what we can reasonably do while waiting for bad weather to pass.

Feelings are just like that. The best way to handle unpleasant feelings is to recognize them (don't try to ignore them or pretend they aren't there), to accept them (you can't control them directly, why try to fight something you can't defeat anyway?), and to go on about doing what you need to do. Rain or fog may not stop you from going to school or to work, but you will take the weather into consideration while driving. In the same way, anxiety need not stop you from studying or asking for a raise in pay, though you'll take it into consideration while selecting a place and time to study or a proper moment to approach your boss. And, in time, unpleasant feelings pass, just like snowstorms. Grief, for example, never sustains its intensity forever. It fades little by little over time unless something comes along to restimulate it again, then it fades again. Just like changeable weather.

As you can see, I'm making a clear distinction between feelings and behavior. Feelings are natural phenomena, uncontrollable directly by our will; they come and go like weather. Behavior (preparing for an interview, for example, or dealing with a difficult client) is controllable. We can choose to dress properly for an interview (behavior) even though we cannot choose to get rid of our anxiety (feeling) about it. We can ask someone out on a date (behavior) while feeling shy. We can total up the check at a restaurant (behavior) even though we cannot choose to avoid our unpleasant feelings about making others wait while we do so. Just as we can decide to go on a picnic even though the day is windy. This distinction between directly controllable behavior and directly uncontrollable feelings is a key feature of Constructive Living action thought.

If we have no direct control over something, we cannot be held responsible for it. Who is responsible for an earthquake? We aren't responsible for having angry, spiteful, depressed, sexy, grumpy, greedy or any other kind of feelings. Again, feelings are natural. On the other hand, we are responsible for what we do, our behavior, no matter what we are feeling. Behavior (except for a few areas like stuttering and sexual impotence and trembling) is controllable by our will, so we are responsible for that aspect of our lives all the time. To be sure, we find it convenient to try to escape from our responsibility for our actions by blaming our feelings. "I was so angry I couldn't help hitting him," "I was too distraught to thank her," "I feel the need for drugs is so strong that I steal to get them." But these feeling-based excuses don't hold water. Similarly, blaming parents or society or spouses or children for our destructive behavior is to seek to avoid responsibility for what is rightfully our own responsibility, no matter what past experiences we may have suffered through.

One of the interesting things about humans is that what we do (our behavior) often influences how we feel. We never have direct control over our natural feelings, but sometimes we can affect our affect by our actions. If you don't feel like going on a job interview one morning it seems to me that it is a waste of time to try to make yourself want to do so. I think it is natural to feel some hesitation about laying your ego on the line for someone else to decide whether you are worthy of hiring or not. There is no need to make yourself enjoy job interviews. The solution? Simply to get out of bed, get dressed for the interview, and go. Sometimes, in the dressing and reading over your resume and driving over to the appointment a sort of excitement and interest in what will happen arises. Sometimes it doesn't. In either case, the interview gets done. Doing a few job interviews well, succeeding at them, having jobs offered to you as a result, may make job hunting even pleasurable. But lying in bed, putting off getting up, and failing to show up for the job interview never gives you a chance to succeed, never gives you a chance to feel anything but uncomfortable about job interviews. The more we allow feelings to govern our lives, the more they spread to govern even larger areas of life.

So we can use our behavior to give ourselves the chance to succeed at accomplishing our goals. And that success often produces confidence and other satisfying feelings.

Pleasant feelings fade over time just as unpleasant ones do, unless something happens to restimulate those feelings. Romantic love fades in a lot of marriages. Respect for individuals and school spirit and patriotic feelings toward one's country can be expected to fade unless restimulated somehow.

That's what dates and rallies and national anthems are about. In the doing of these things certain feelings are likely to be stimulated or restimulated. If you want to keep love in your relationship you must keep doing kindness for your partner. As you behave in thoughtful, loving ways you are increasing the chances of sustaining feelings of love for him or her. Romance in a marriage is sustained by gifts and candle-lit dinners and kisses and dressing up for each other and so forth.

But even this focus on influencing feelings indirectly through behavior is a bit unnatural. Sometimes you seem to do everything right, you plan the proper behaviors to generate certain feelings, and the feelings don't turn out as expected. A better strategy for living is to be purpose-focused instead of being feeling-focused. Let the feelings take care of themselves while you go about accomplishing your goals through your behavior. As the emphasis in your life turns more and more toward using controllable behavior to achieve your goals life steadies down and becomes more satisfying. I am not talking here of the tunnel vision workaholic who focuses only on business and economic success. Purposes and goals are various. But, on the whole, being purpose-oriented will pay off more than being feeling-oriented simply because the latter isn't a game you can win with any consistency. You can't make good feelings last and last; you can't make bad feelings go away at will. (Technically, it isn't proper to use words like "good" and "bad" when referring to feelings; like seasons, they have no moral qualities.)

If feelings are natural phenomena doesn't it seem strange to you that there are psychotherapies which try to make fears or guilt or depression go away? There are psychotherapies and self growth methods which aim at producing happiness and confidence and good feelings about yourself all the time. I cannot see how such therapies can deliver on their promises. No one is happy or confident or feeling good about anything all the time. Feelings keep changing, like the sky keeps changing. A more suitable goal for therapy or for human life in general seems to be to notice and accept these changes in feelings while keeping steadily on about doing the things that will get us where we want to go. Like water does.

Morita therapy holds that all humans are oversensitive to their own faults and limits to some degree. Especially when we are ill or under stress we may become fixated on some mental/physical disturbance. We blow out of proportion the ringing in our ears or our stiff shoulders or our fear of flying or our discomfort about eating in restaurants or whatever. The proper course to alleviate these problem areas is not to ignore them or to fight them, but to accept them while getting on about proper, constructive behavior. In other words, whatever is troubling us, it is important to accept the troubled feelings and get on about living. Of course, if there is something practical and concrete we can do to alleviate the cause of the problem (such as seeing a physician to rule out organic illness), that is included in the category of proper, constructive behavior.

In general, the stronger we desire something, the more we want to succeed, the greater our anxiety about failure. Our worries and fears are reminders of the strength of our positive desires. They are also reminders of our needs to use caution, prepare materials to avoid the embarrassment of lack of preparation, work hard, practice perfecting our skills, develop our ability to persist and endure, deal with the environmental circumstances which caused them, and so forth. Our anxieties are indispensable for us in spite of the discomfort accompanying them. To try to do away with them would be foolish. Morita therapy is not really a psychotherapeutic method for getting rid of "symptoms." It is more an educational method for outgrowing our self-imposed limitations. Through Constructive Living we learn to accept the naturalness of ourselves.

In their advanced stages Constructive Living students accept themselves as part of the natural situation in which they are embedded. I do not refer to some passive conformity, but to a dynamic recognition that we exist as situationally-embedded aspects of Reality. We take on our identities from the circumstances in which we find ourselves. We are rather like the cursor markers on the computer screen of Reality. The loss of self-centeredness, in more than one sense of the word, is an ultimate goal for some students of this method. However, relief from the obsessive pressure of phobias, anxieties, and psychosomatic difficulties is sufficient for many students.

What we have considered here so far has come from the thought of the Japanese psychiatrist, Shoma Morita (or Masatake Morita; Japanese kanji characters can be read in various ways. I have placed the family names last in this book to conform with our English custom). Now let's turn briefly to the contribution to Constructive Living made by the lay priest, Ishin Yoshimoto, and his Constructive Living reciprocity.

Constructive Living reciprocity

One of the factors that seems to influence how we feel is our attitude toward the world. If we are constantly concerned with getting our share, with making sure we aren't left out, if we are extremely self-focused and self-conscious, then we are likely to have a lot of miserable feelings. The world just never seems to send us green lights and lottery prizes and kind words when we want them. And we want them nearly all the time.

Have you ever stopped to think about how much of you is truly yours? Your name was given to you by your parents. So was your body. The words you use were taught to you by parents and peers and teachers. Your body has grown and is sustained by food that people you don't even know produced and processed for you. The clothes you wear were created and sewn by others, bought with money given you by someone else. Even the ideas you have seem to bubble to the surface of your mind, coming out of nowhere and passing along to be replaced by other thoughts from nowhere. There's nothing that is truly yours; it is all borrowed. Of course, it is the same for all of us.

You may say, of course, that you bought your clothes with your own money. But who gave you the money? Who taught you to do the work you do which earned the money? Who hired you? Who gave you the basic educational skills to learn the trade you ply? The point is that when we trace back our achievements far enough we see the fruits of others' efforts in our behalf, inevitably. We have done nothing solely on our own.

Strange, then, that we should have the notion that we are "self-made." We believe that we got where we are by our own efforts. With just a little bit of reflection we can see that such notions of having come this far on our own are laughable. Deeper reflection allows us to see in even greater detail how we have been and continue to be supported on all sides in all sorts of ways by people and things and energies (such as electricity and the sun's heat and light).

One result of sorting out the specific, concrete ways in which the world supports us (just as you are supporting me now by loaning me your eyes to read this chapter) is a feeling of gratitude. I don't deserve all this help from you and this paper and the electricity that powers this word processor (and the people who worked to generate this electricity), and the editor and publisher of this book, and the manufacturers of this printer's ink, book designers, and the people who taught me these lifeways, and so forth. But, through Constructive Living reciprocity, we can come to notice and appreciate the surrounding nurturance from the world and to offer words of thanks. Before I underwent a week of Constructive Living reciprocity training in Japan, I thought all this was my due. I took it for granted, and drift back into that attitude sometimes still. But whether I recognize it or not, whether I accept it or not, whether I feel gratitude or not, whether I try to return the favors or not, Reality keeps on being what it is. It keeps on giving to me, not in some abstract sense, but concretely, through Jim and Frank and Lynn and this keyboard and so forth.

So the natural response to realizing what is really going on is the desire to repay and a sort of guilt when we see that we haven't been doing much repaying right along. Starting with our parents our attitude shifts from how little we have received from them and how much more they owe us to one of how much we have received from them and how important it is to start working on giving back something to them. I'm not suggesting that all parents are perfect and that they have done a perfect job in raising us. But I am asserting that there were some adults in our lives who fed and clothed us and nurtured us when we were small. They did it whether they were in the mood or not, over and over again, whether we felt appreciative or showed them gratitude or not--or we wouldn't have survived to be here today.

The gratitude and desire to repay apply to the people in your life today, as well, and to objects in your world. What have you done for your shoes lately, for your car, for electricity, for your toothbrush and stereo set? If you take a moment to consider what they have done for you, it seems not quite so odd to think of what you might do for them in return.

I've never met a suffering neurotic person who was filled with gratitude. Isn't that something? Gratitude and neurotic suffering seem to be antagonistic. If there is anything characteristic of neurosis it is a self-centeredness. Gratitude, on the other hand, is other-centered. It carries with it the desire to serve others in repayment, even if it causes some inconvenience to oneself.

The most joyful people I have known have all been people who gave themselves away to others. The most miserable people I have known have all been concerned with looking out for themselves. Check with your own experience, look around.

Despite commercials to the contrary, looking out for number one is a sure path to torment.

On Being Natural

When we say that the weather is terrible or that it is a pleasant day we are really talking about our convenience and our preference and not about some moral quality of the weather. The weather just is. It is cloudy or drizzly or foggy or clear or nippy or whatever. It is what nature presents to us at a particular time. We must take the weather into account when we dress to go out in it, when we plan a picnic, when we decide what tires to put on the car, when we decide whether to carry an umbrella to work. Nevertheless, the weather doesn't force us to make any particular decision about what we shall do. For example, we may choose to wear a swimsuit in the rain and wash our car in a drizzle, we may continue with our picnic plans even though it is windy, we may decide that snow tires are too expensive to buy, and we may prefer to run to the car rather than use an umbrella.

The weather is part of the natural reality that is presented to us for our consideration. So are feelings. Being afraid of heights is just as natural as a breezy autumn day; so is nervousness when we are about to meet new and important people in our lives. Anxiety before taking an examination, concern while waiting for medical laboratory reports on our physical condition, embarrassment when we have made a blunder in front of others, grief when a loved one (or a job) is lost--all these feelings are as natural as the weather.

When we try to single out some feelings as "terrible" or "unwarranted" or "intrusive" or "hindering" or "beneath us," we are likely to forget their proper naturalness. When we recognize their essential innocence we can go on about life, simply acknowledging their existence as we acknowledge a foggy morning. It is sensible to try to work our way around fog--we use dimmed headlights, drive slower, and so forth. Anyone who tries to attack the fog directly seems foolish to us. It does no good to slash away at fog with a sword or a fan. Why, then, do we try to get rid of our fears and anxieties? Why is the purpose of some psychotherapies to try to free the patients from worries and self-doubts and apprehensions? I suspect that some therapists try this impossible task not only because their patients are distressed by their feelings (some people are distressed by gloomy weather, too), but also because the therapists and patients have the mistaken notion that the feelings somehow interfere with the patients' doing what they need to do in life.

We commonly say, for example, that Mr. X won't fly on an airplane because he is afraid of flying. We may even believe that Mr. X's fear causes him to refrain from flying. It isn't so. It can't be so, because there are plenty of people who fear flying (I am one of them) and yet travel by plane all the time. Perhaps, you say, it is the degree of fear that distinguishes between people who fly and people who don't. I wonder. I used to be very, very frightened (much more than I am now) and still flew because there was no other reasonable way to get from Los Angeles to Japan and back in the time available.

In the psychology of suicide we often talk about persons who are too depressed to be suicidal. The danger of suicide comes when their depression begins to lift. While they are at the bottom of depression they have no energy to plan or act on their suicidal plan. So it is not the feeling of depression that causes people to kill themselves. Throughout human life, it is simply impossible to make a clear, simple causal connection between what we feel and what we do. When we look closely at feelings and behavior we see some correlation (like the correlation between the number of umbrellas we see on the street and rain clouds in the sky) but no simple causal relationship (just as we see some people without umbrellas even though it is raining).

I do not know what causes us to do what we do. I really don't. I know that it isn't simply feelings. I suspect that no one else is certain about what causes us to act as we do, either, although some claim such awesome insight. It seems clear, however, that when we get to the point of accepting our feelings as we accept the inevitability of the weather, when we take into consideration the information about our feelings as we consider the information in a weather report, and then go ahead with what we have decided needs to be done, we end up in better shape than those who shake their fists at the clouds in the sky or scream at (or ignore) the weather reports.

You see, even the most unpleasant feelings are the natural result of our wanting to live and to live fully. The fear of meeting others grows from the desire to be liked and respected by them. The fear of heights is self-preserving, reflecting a reluctance to put ourselves in dangerous situations. Self-criticism and feelings of inferiority indicate a strong desire to improve ourselves. We compare ourselves with real or imagined others, noticing their apparent abilities and successes.

Our skill at observation and our strong drive to succeed are reflected in our self-doubts. People who don't care about living successfully don't have worries about job interviews and examinations; they don't have inferiority feelings; they don't suffer from shyness or lack of confidence. Those who don't care are to be pitied. If we grow beyond the petty human feelings and concerns then we lose empathy and sympathy for other suffering humans. It is far better to continue to feel while developing better discipline in our behavior. In this way, we don't lose our membership in humanity, though we advance up the ranks of character.

The "natural" person, then, simply takes the feelings as they come, all intertwined and interacting, and goes about doing what reality brings that needs doing. The "natural" person wastes no time trying to struggle with feelings directly. The feelings are just "ordinary," unworthy of lots of attention over a long period of time. Feelings shouldn't be ignored--how could we ignore a snowstorm, anyway? But when you have to go out in a blizzard, you go out. That is the way it is to be human. The feelings are there, but we do what we have to do. Even in summer, when the ice hasn't melted, shivering, we do what we have to do.

Sometimes This, Sometimes That

I dislike being told how I must be feeling. Locked out of my office one day I remember feeling inconvenienced but not particularly angry. A colleague insisted that I must have been angry--after all, someone had forgotten to tell me about the change of locks. But I wasn't angry, I insisted. Sometimes I'm angry, to be sure, but not that time. He persisted: I must have been very angry to deny and repress it so strongly. I wonder.

Sometimes we feel pressured by psychological theory or by friends or therapists or spouses to own up to emotions that they insist must be there. When someone pulls out from the curb in front of my car without any signal and I am forced to brake suddenly, then sometimes I am upset and sometimes not. There seems to be no purpose in digging for anger that someone else believes must be hidden somewhere in my psyche. If I am denying and repressing the feeling, why do I recognize and affirm it sometimes? Why should I try to fit my experience to someone else's theoretical satisfaction?

It is the same with speaking before large audiences. Sometimes I am more tense than at other times. Sometimes I feel more courageous and less shy than at other times. Aren't you the same? When we reflect back on our childhood, weren't we sometimes angry at our parents and sometimes appreciative of them, sometimes satisfied with our lot and sometimes intensely dissatisfied, sometimes loving and sometimes hating? To talk about an unhappy childhood is to oversimplify the complexity of the past in order to fit some current need. We may want to consider ourselves deprived as children so that we can explain our current limitations. We may want to emphasize our feelings of abandonment as children in order to please some sort of counselor who, we hope, can ultimately make some organized sense of our lives. I wonder.

The simplified explanations of life built upon uncaring fathers and overprotective mothers and expectable feelings may have some value because they make us believe that we have a handle on why we are the way we are. But they aren't true. I'm really very sorry to put it so bluntly. They aren't true. They are simple fairy tales about who we were and are. The reality is so much richer and more complex than these caricatures that a little genuine reflection will show them to be imaginative scaffolds for reconstructing a safely understandable past. There may very well have been an overprotective mother in your past. But her existence is no single-variable explanation of your lack of self-confidence or your current difficulties with your office pals or your fights with the kids. What you felt then and what you feel now and what you will feel tomorrow are so complexly determined (as much by what you have done as by what others have done to you) that to buy into any simple psychodynamic explanatory system is rather childlike and naive.

It occurs to me that the news media have helped perpetuate these oversimplified views of ourselves and our world. When I am interviewed on television the newsperson or talk show host wants to know *the single* problem with mental hospitals. What is *the* cause of neurotic suffering? What are *the three reasons* why people kill themselves? Broadcast time and print space are limited. The complexities of reality aren't what people want to hear and read--or so many media people seem to think. Television, radio, and newspapers seem always to need something immediate, something unusual. News shows meet that need, as do sports events and call-in shows with topical themes. Such programming is ephemeral. It isn't expected to provide in-depth, lasting information. Instead, it will soon be replaced by spot reporting of other recent events. The long term view, the history, the panorama, are relegated to a brief background statement. The result is an oversimplification in our understanding and in our approach to understanding. But there is a different area in which simplification is not only possible, but desirable.

Consider the possibility of simply accepting the feelings and moods and emotional reactions to events as they are. No need to try to make rational sense of them. No need to fathom their historical roots. No need to pause to reflect on whether they are normal or not. No need to examine what you ought to be feeling according to someone else's expectation. It is strange to call this perspective radical. But in this day and age it is radical to consider feelings to be natural phenomena, like temperature changes or leaves falling from trees in autumn. We would prefer that feelings be more like traffic lights-- predictable, controllable, and dependable if we pace our lives properly and rationally. But the experience of emotion isn't mechanical in any simple way, like a traffic light. To try to exert direct control over our feelings based on some psychological understanding is, in any exact sense, fruitless.

So where does that perspective leave us? Are we destined to be buffeted about by every emotional gust? Can we make no sense at all of why we feel as we do? Are we doomed to passive resignation in the area of feelings? Not at all. Whatever perspective we adopt intellectually, we all continue to make some rough sense of why we are grouchy this morning, why we are tense when greeting the mailman today, why the tears came to our eyes during that movie episode. Our attempts to understand give us ideas about what we need to do in our lives, what needs to be changed in order to reduce or increase the likelihood of certain feelings. Nevertheless, there is a great deal of slippage between what we understand about our feelings and what actually causes the feelings. And there is slippage again between what we understand about our feelings and what we can and will do about the conditions that contribute to them. What I am arguing for here is, I suppose, a sort of humility about our feelings. With all our fine psychological theories we sometimes delude ourselves into believing that we really know a great deal about what is going on in our emotional lives. The emotional lives of not a few psychotherapists and counselors in my acquaintance belie this belief. We know very little.

What is certain is that I am sometimes this, sometimes that. Sometimes pleased, sometimes not; sometimes confident, sometimes not; sometimes compassionate, sometimes not. The ice doesn't melt at my whim. It doesn't melt no matter how well I understand its origins or believe I understand its origins. It may not melt despite my persistent efforts to change the circumstances that I believe to be maintaining it. In such cases what else is there to do but shiver and go on about living?

Given that the above perspective more accurately describes what is going on in our affective or emotional lives, why go to the trouble to consider feelings from this unusual point of view? First, we no longer need to waste effort and energy trying for some elaborate intellectual insight. Some people will opt to seek psychodynamic insight whether it is practically useful or not, simply because it is interesting. No problem there. Positive and creative results can come to those who play with the symbols of the psyche. But that is not an endeavor of "cure," it is exploration. Second, the energy once devoted to seeking deep understanding of the hidden self can be redirected toward the more workable and controllable aspect of life--what we do. It isn't nearly as much fun to dig in and clean up our behavioral act, but the results are gratifying and dependable.

As a consequence of adopting this perspective on feelings we begin to accept them rather than trying to control, create, or dissolve them. We begin to see them as natural consequences of events sometimes recognized and sometimes not, but always natural. Natural means not good or bad, just natural. When a lion kills and devours its prey it may not be a pretty sight, but the lion isn't bad for doing what it is natural for lions to do. Lions haven't the rational, thoughtful control over behavior that we humans can choose to assert over our own acts. A depression may be painful to endure and hurtful to watch in someone else, but the hopeless and sorrow-filled feelings aren't bad. They are natural. We may use medication to ease the suffering (just as we may feed a caged lion), but there remains a degree of suffering that must be lived with while one gets on about shoveling away the snow on one's doorstep. And remarkably often, when we get involved in the shoveling, we lose sight of the sorrow and hopelessness.

This new point of view allows a freedom and self-acceptance of great depth. My feelings are an aspect of me. I don't need to understand them fully or to "solve" or to "dissolve" them somehow in order to get on with my life. I am the way I am, naturally. While working to improve my behavior there is no need to struggle with the doubts and obsessions and despair. They are all natural, just as they are. They aren't my responsibility; they are just passing through. I am not substandard or abnormal for having these thoughts and feelings. They are all right as they are. I am all right as I am. Now to get on with shoveling the walk.

The Essence of Constructive Living

What are the absolutely essential elements of Constructive Living? What defines it as a unique lifeway or therapeutic method? How does one know whether a technique fits within the framework of Constructive Living?

Let me say a few words about what is not essential to Constructive Living. As far as I can see there are some characteristic techniques but no specific techniques that are essential. We can do Constructive Living without doing absolute bedrest as in Japan's inpatient Morita therapy and without seated meditation as in Japan's Constructive Living reciprocity. We can do Constructive Living without diary guidance or reading assignments.

There is nothing particularly Japanese about Constructive Living. It isn't necessary to use foreign words like *shinkeishitsu* or *toraware* or even Morita or Yoshimoto. There is no requirement that our students be interested in Zen or things Japanese.

So what is left? As far as I can see there are a few essential principles, orientations, and a small class of techniques that constitute the core of Constructive Living.

1. Principles.
a. Reality focus.

Reality must be accepted as it is. Feelings are a natural part of reality. It follows that they must be accepted, without direct struggle.

Both the action element of Constructive Living (from Morita therapy) and the reciprocity element of Constructive Living (from Naikan therapy) ask us to look at reality. They are realistic. And both lead us to act on reality. It isn't enough to ponder, to ruminate, to intellectualize, to imagine. We must take what we know into the world and apply it in order to keep learning, growing, living.

Some suffering in the world is based on real problems. Some suffering is based on excessive self-focus and experiential ignorance. The solution to the latter suffering is experience-based education.

The essential goal of Constructive Living is to see reality clearly. We haven't paid proper attention (Constructive Living action), have inadvertently misperceived it (Constructive Living action), or have selfishly misperceived it (Constructive Living reciprocity).

A side effect of Constructive Living action may be reduction in symptoms or suffering. It may be a new appreciation of the colors and variety in nature. A side effect of Constructive Living reciprocity may be gratitude or guilt or some other feeling. It may be a resolve to repay the world or clean up one's life or sweep the sidewalk. But both require us to recognize and encounter specific, concrete, detailed reality. They discourage overuse of abstraction, generalization, and vagueness.

   b. Action/experiential orientation
   Constructive Living emphasizes the need to put what is learned into life activity every day. Constructive Living action and Constructive Living reciprocity aren't strategies which ultimately remove us from the world into some non-productive withdrawn existence. They are at their best and most useful as we operate in everyday life.

   Behavior is the controllable aspect of reality. It is through purposeful, realistic behavior that we work to change reality. We are responsible for what we do no matter what we feel. A few phenomena (some people include them in the category of behaviors) such as stuttering, trembling, and impotence are not directly controllable by the will. They are considered to be uncontrollable expressions of feelings and must be accepted as they are while the student works on controllable behaviors.

   Attention must be focused on reality. Reality is the proper teacher of life's lessons. Observation of reality results in information about what needs to be done (i.e., purposeful behavior). When what needs to be done isn't clear Constructive Living action can suggest only to do what is clear. That is part of the reason for the structured nature of Zen monasteries. One's situation, when properly structured, presents what needs doing in relatively routine and clear fashion so that attention can be invested in doing activities well. The simple and organized life reduces the attention necessary for deciding what needs doing.

The Constructive Living approach to the issue of knowing what needs doing includes the organization and simplification of Morita and Zen but also the moral investigation of Constructive Living reciprocity. Constructive Living reciprocity introspection helps us to discover, even in the most complex situation, what needs to be done. Constructive Living reciprocity provides a moral compass for determining what needs to be done. Then the Constructive Living action practice helps us become people who actually do it.

Intellectual understanding may be helpful on some level, but action-grounded experiential understanding is of greater dependability and benefit. Action on Reality teaches Truth. Reflection on the past and planning for the future may provide useful insights and valuable preparations, but excessive rumination and daydreaming are self-centered and harmful.

c. No self.

Constructive Living shows us no-self. Constructive Living action shows how we merge with our environments. We are Reality's way of getting Reality's work done. As we fit ourselves to the situations we encounter we become the situations, harmonized in a way that reduces conflict and misery.

d. Foundation of religion.

Both Morita and Yoshimoto remarked that their therapies aren't religion, but that they direct us to the foundation of the religious impulse. We become a better Christians or Jews or

Muslims or Buddhists for having studied these lifeways. Questions such as the following commonly arise from putting Constructive Living principles into long practice: Why does the world take care of me even though I am imperfect, make mistakes, cause others discomfort? What causes me to want to succeed, to criticize myself when I fail, to worry about success? Why do purposes emerge in my mind to direct my behavior? Such questions can be considered religious questions. Neither the action aspect of Constructive Living nor the reciprocity aspect of Constructive Living attempts to provide answers to such questions.

2. Orientations

a. The lifeway, not the teacher

Both Constructive Living action and Constructive Living reciprocity emphasize the method and not the teacher. They direct us to develop our own potential without dependence on some other person with supposedly superior powers. The instructor is merely a guide, a sounding board, an advisor. Zen teachers, too, talk about the finger pointing at the moon. "I'm only the pointing finger," they say, "not the moon. Don't confuse the two."

Characteristic orientations mark the teacher/practitioner of Constructive Living. Most notable is the lack of separation between the teacher's life and the lifeway he or she teaches. Constructive Living is not an approach to helping others that is used only in the office setting. It permeates the life.

b. Educational model

The model underlying the practice of Constructive Living is educational, not medical. We prefer to use terms such as "student," "teacher," "guidance," "habit," "graduation," and the like to terms such as "patient," "therapist," "healing," "symptom," and "cure."

Acceptance is a key attitude modeled by the teacher/guide. Genuine acceptance naturally leads to gratitude and a desire to serve others. Constructive action is a natural part of the whole. The guide is reality-centered, reality-confident.

During the teaching sessions the guide is constantly engaged in turning the student's attention toward reality.

3. Representative techniques

Characteristic techniques are employed in Constructive Living, but perhaps no single technique is essential. Any method that promotes the student's constructive learning from reality may be used.

Experiential assignments such as cleaning a public park or telephoning for a job interview or writing a letter of thanks or shopping for fresh vegetables may be made. Daily journal assignments are common with multiple columns and behaviors recorded separately from feelings.

A detailed review of recent behaviors and their results and quizzes about the details of surroundings help redirect the student's attention away from feeling-centered self focus.

Constructive Living instructors often use the principle of yielding, more or less as it is used in the martial arts. Rather than meeting the force of the student's misconceptions head-on, the instructor uses the student's own energy, deflecting it in a desired direction. For example, "You say that you are a perfectionist, but you aren't nearly perfectionistic enough. You haven't noticed the fire exits in this room. Be more perfectionistic in your observation of your surroundings." "You complain of guilt, but what you do to cause the guilt hasn't changed. You need more guilt." With these unexpected remarks and the subsequent changes in behavior, the student comes to view mental states as acceptable as they are.

The teacher/guide may listen, advise, offer koans for reflection, assign readings, take walks with the student, go shopping with the student, help clean the student's room and office, attend the student's wedding ceremony. Always the teacher reflects reality back to the student and encourages the student to recognize it and act on it positively.

Conclusion

Other teachers of Constructive Living might emphasize different aspects of the practice, but I submit that we would agree on these core concepts and methods. It is reassuring that in order to teach this lifeway to others we need not be perfect provided we are Realistic.

What it is that We Teach

Constructive Living is overtly a teaching practice. As a guide, I have something to teach my students: namely, a way to live that will relieve unnecessary suffering. It is important to listen to the students' problems and perspectives so that the teaching can be tailored to their needs and explained so that they will be able to understand and be able to try out principles in real experience. There is much to learn in a session. There is no time for the time filler "How do you feel about that?" unless the student is specifically having trouble recognizing and accepting feelings. Complaints and rambling descriptions of emotional ups and downs are discouraged. The goal of Constructive Living is not understanding the distant historical source of our troubling emotions.

Some people believe that when they have some understanding of the childhood origins of their feelings they will have control over them. That impression isn't realistic. We have no control over them unless that knowledge leads to changes of attention and behavior. Insight alone is, for many, a way of avoiding making the effortful, sometimes painful, changes in behavior that are necessary to produce changed feelings and an improved concept of one's self.

Thus it seems reasonable to accept one's feelings as they are (rather than using energy and attention trying to analyze them) and get right to work on attention and behavior. However, such acceptance is not passive; we still work to change our circumstances for the better. We still make efforts to improve the lot of those around us. But the inner turmoil is gone. The conflict within is no more. It is no longer me opposing this condition. It becomes me here doing this. That is all. That is sufficient.

The doing is what is important, not the result. From the Constructive Living action point of view, no act is merely instrumental. Every act is an end in itself. The quality of our attention in action is crucial. Sometimes I work hard and nothing seems to come of the results of the work. I may put in a lot of time weeding, for example, only to find a new crop of weeds springing up within a week. Or a raging forest fire might destroy the cabin that took years to build. However, nothing can take away the changes in my character that resulted from my full attention to that weeding or the building of that cabin. With every fully attended activity I am working not only on the project at hand but on myself as well. Behavior is what counts. Not emotion. Not even the results of behavior. What I do is the only thing in life that I can control. No one can guarantee a life of good feelings. No one can guarantee that our efforts will bring the results that we hope for. We must be clear on what is doable and what is not.

It seems that most folks most of the time simply get through life. Their days are spent merely passing time until the weekends or until their vacations. They mark a few outstanding events--graduation day, the trip to Hawaii, the day they got married, the birth of a child--but the rest of life is unremarkable and without particular meaning for them. How much richer, it seems to me, to be able to think of every day as important, every act as rich with meaning. Such an attitude allows one to live life instead of merely enduring it.

In the Constructive Living action context, every act provides the opportunity for purposeful accomplishment and personal growth. Every act can involve moments of directed attention. Pouring a cup of coffee, scrubbing the bathtub, writing a thank-you note, arranging the pages of a photo album, signaling a left turn, setting an alarm, kissing a loved one--all these activities can be, should be, carried out with the clear focus and scrupulous care they deserve. All we have is that flow of attention. If we do not use it with awareness, if we do not recognize its pervasive nature, then we misuse the only treasure we have, we lose life.

To be sure, it is easier to put out the effort when you come to understand something about yourself, when you have an emotional high, when you enjoy the meal your life partner cooked, when you choose life rather than self-destruction. But no one else causes these choices and experiences for you. No one else controls them. No one else controls you. Your responsibility, your control, lies only in the sphere of your own behavior. What results is up to you and reality. Being in charge of yourself is a full-time job.

Responsibility is an important topic for consideration here. It is critical to distinguish between understanding and condoning. The former has nothing to do with responsibility; the latter assigns it elsewhere. Western psychotherapy, in its attempt to understand disturbed behavior, bends over backward and ends up condoning or excusing hurtful, destructive acts. Look at all the extenuating psychological circumstances that affect our criminal justice system's decisions. In Constructive Living we are quite clear on the boundary between understanding and condoning. We seek to understand and condone any feeling, any feeling at all. The desire to kill or steal, fear, shyness, panic, sexual attraction, disgust, pride, joy, reverence, and so forth are all equally acceptable, that is, to be accepted as they are. There is nothing wrong with any of these feelings. They are not acts. They may cause us discomfort, but they don't directly affect anyone else.

On the other hand, we seek to understand, but refuse to condone, any harmful behavior, no matter what the confused and powerful feelings that lie behind them. Behavior is the only way we directly affect other people. To feel like killing another human is natural in some circumstances; to actually kill another human is wrong. I may want to understand what is going through the mind of a murderer before the crime, but, whatever he is thinking or feeling, the murder cannot be condoned. It is quite a relief, actually, when we realize that we have no responsibility for our feelings. They are uncontrollable; they are natural; they need only be accepted as they are. Still, we must take clear responsibility for what we do, and we must hold others responsible for what they do. If we fail to do so, we run the risk of just the sorts of injustices that appear in the name of justice in our courts every day.

When the courts punish parents for a crime committed by their children, the reason for the punishment should not be that they are responsible for their children's behavior. They are not. Each of us is responsible for his or her own behavior, even children. The punishment is justified because of the parents' improper parenting. Their behavior was at fault and not their lack of control over their children's behavior. Can you see how important the difference is? To hold one of us responsible for another's behavior is meaningless for the one and demeaning for the other. I simply cannot control what you do. You cannot be absolved of responsibility for what you do. It is as simple as that.

II. Constructive Living and Feelings

Moving Ahead

When you awaken at four A.M. and can't go back to sleep, what do you do? When you are angered and frustrated by injustices committed by powerful people in your life, what do you do? Notice that even if you understand the reasons for the sleeplessness or for the anger, the conditions don't go away. Even if you make every effort to will yourself to be sleepy or to be calm, you cannot.

While you are feeling bad, when life isn't turning out as you wish it would, it is much better to accept the insomnia and the anger while directing your efforts toward doing what is useful, productive, and constructive. At four A.M., why not read a magazine or write letters? How about an early-morning walk or shopping at an all-night supermarket? These activities are much more interesting than the inner struggle to conquer insomnia. It's not fair! you moan. Other people sleep through the night. So you lie there in discomfort, tossing about, now too warm, now too cold, feeling depressed. Then eventually you arise more tired than ever. Life need not include these useless struggles when you learn which parts of yourself to pamper and allow their own way and which parts to control by your own direction.

The other day I was working with my personal computer, trying to get it to print something stored in its memory. I made some entries from the keyboard, but nothing happened. I tried another set of entries; still it didn't work. I tried repeating the process, pushing the keys again and again. How annoying! It ought to work! I found myself pushing harder on the keys in an attempt to exert my will on the computer. But it wasn't programmed to function in that way. The computer didn't care that I was angry and trying to impose my will on it.

Realizing my foolishness, I tried yet another way to get around the obstacle, and this time everything ran smoothly. Fascinating! It was necessary to discover the proper action, then all proceeded in an orderly fashion. No matter how intent and determined I was, no matter how much I desired the result, no matter how emotional or how cool I tried to become, the computer responded only to my actions. Until I did what needed to be done, the results were unsatisfactory.

Like the computer, the world about me responds to my behavior. It can't feel my feelings. Reality doesn't respond to my will or my wishes or my emotions. To believe that positive thinking changes the world directly is childlike naivete. To be sure, my thoughts and feelings may influence what I do (my behavior), and that action, in turn, may influence reality. But it is what I do that affects my world. And it is the same for you.

It follows that if you want to make changes in your marriage or in your job or in your grades at school or in your character, you must change what you are doing. You don't need to change how you feel about something to affect it. For example, if you want closer ties with your spouse, you don't need to begin by loving him or her more. If you want to have more friends, you don't have to begin by feeling less shy or more self-confident. Changes *begin* with action.

Feelings are for Feeling

You won't see me cry in public. It's not that I'm cold and insensitive. It's not that I'm suppressing feelings or ignoring them or pretending I'm not feeling what I am. I have a choice whether to let others in on what I'm feeling. Mostly I choose not to do so. When I cry, I'd prefer to be alone.

Some men these days are being criticized by factions of women and other men for not being expressive of their emotions. Those criticisms are based on unrealistic assumptions. Here are a few of them:

Critics assume that the only two possibilities for handling feelings is to express them or suppress them. The third alternative--recognizing them, acknowledging them without external expression, and getting on with doing what needs doing-- isn't considered, even though that third alternative is the one we all utilize most of the time.

Critics don't seem to realize that both sexes hold back expression of feelings most of the time. We cannot be bothered with expressing every feeling which pops up in our psyches, nor do others wish to be bothered with an ongoing report of our fluctuating mood state. It would be a burden on others to have to put up with a stream of messages about our feelings. We all hide our feelings, if you will. If you look closely at the complaints about non-expression of feelings by males you will see that the critics call for the increased expression of only certain kinds of feelings in certain circumstances. Anger, sorrow, vulnerability, and the like are primarily targeted. I have never understood why these particular feelings should be displayed for others on demand. I suspect that the attempt to coerce males into expressing these feelings in social contexts is an attempt at some sort of social leveling, a distorted effort by the critics to get some social confirmation of their own feelings. But feeling any feeling is all right. We don't need to be reassured that others have these feelings, too. They do.

I continue to be intrigued that people believe they have secret feelings known only to mental health professionals who are capable of putting their clients in touch with those feelings. That belief is not so different from believing that anyone could be unwittingly possessed by devils which can be exorcised by some religious professionals. Interestingly, the feelings which we are supposed to have lurking in our psyches are uniformly unpleasant ones. Why can't we get in touch with our hidden joy? Why can't we discover we've been happy all these years without knowing it? Sounds sort of foolish doesn't it? If such a psychotherapy doesn't exist already, it is probably on its way.

With rare exceptions Western psychotherapy doesn't value individual experience while claiming that it does. What it values is *interpreted* individual experience. The interpretation must be provided by or at least validated by a mental health professional. Rather than acknowledging the full implications of feelings, for example, much of Western psychological counseling seems to trivialize and discount feelings. When feelings are considered to be merely markers of past parental mistakes or signs of current psychological diagnostic categories or indications of the working of the unconscious (or other mystical, untestable constructions) then the feelings themselves are primarily tokens of "more important" phenomena. It is important to recognize the value of the experienced feeling itself and the information it brings. When one is engaged in fighting a feeling or "curing" its cause the focus remains on escape. In order to derive full benefit from a feeling it must be accepted, incorporated into momentary life experience, not resisted.

It increasingly appears that much of Western psychological counseling (both psychodynamic and behavioral) aims at little more than distraction from genuine and natural emotions through specialized cognitive maneuvering. It is time that we stopped trying to "fix" feelings and got on with the more important and practical objective of feeling feelings and learning from them while engaging in purposeful behavior.

Some day we'll learn that feelings, any and all feelings, are for feeling.

Alternatives for Indulgence

In the Western world we went from emotional illiteracy to an obsessive concern of emotions over the period of a hundred years or so, especially as a result of Freud's influence. The feeling focus of modern culture covers laziness, sloppy thinking, rationalization, and self indulgence. Maybe there was a time when many people didn't recognize what they were feeling much of the time, but now there is an overemphasis on feelings as the most important element of human life. Some people seem to be attending primarily to their own feelings, building their lives around them. What we need these days is not to get in touch with feelings, but to go beyond the reality of feelings alone, and to get in touch with the larger reality of circumstances.

Consider how the word "feeling" has spilled over its natural boundaries into other areas of human existence. Some speakers say, "I feel like a hamburger for lunch." Others say, "I feel that she did commit the crime." In Japan a major advertising campaign centered on the phrase "I feel Coke." Psychotherapists use the very convenient time-filler query, "And how do you feel about that?" How lazy we have become! How undisciplined in thought and behavior!

Constructive Living doesn't ask anyone to give up feeling. But we must beware of overindulging the feeling side of our lives. When we focus on emotions exclusively other important aspects of living are neglected. We must balance our awareness of feelings with attentive, purposeful action in the world. "Every man feels instinctively that all the beautiful sentiments in the world weigh less than a single lovely action," wrote James Russell Lowell.

Constructive Living recommends that we attend to even the smallest tasks of daily life with mindful attention. Some see a danger that Constructive Living might turn attention to trivial, insignificant acts allowing an escape from important human tasks. I doubt it. There may be short-term escape from some of life's unpleasantness by focusing on doing daily life well, but we eventually tire of escaping into other life tasks. There is something in us humans that calls us to more than triviality.

Until recently we seemed to have the two alternatives of (1)individual freedom with all the concomitant social ills--teen age suicides, violence, crime, unwanted pregnancies, social unrest-- or (2)social control with increasing restrictions to protect and control. Now, through Constructive Living, we are offered a third possibility of freedom in the areas that are genuinely free and self control in the areas that require personal and social responsibility. Constructive Living doesn't make it easy to give up smoking; it doesn't produce laws that make it difficult to smoke. It merely tells you that the desire to smoke is uncontrollable and that, regardless of that desire, you smoke or you don't. Notice that there is no talk here of deciding to give up smoking or making a commitment to quit smoking or getting motivated to stop smoking. You stop or you don't. That is reality. The rest is just smoke-talk.

Before, it seemed that we had the alternative of expressing feelings or suppressing them. The alternatives were couched in terms of open honest portrayal of emotions or dishonest unhealthy censoring of them. As noted above, the third alternative presented by Constructive Living is honest recognition and acceptance of feelings without the requirement of behavioral expression of them.

Over the past twenty-five years reality has demonstrated that Constructive Living is not only an effective method for coping with the suffering of existing neuroses, but it can be used to prevent neurosis and minimize the negative effects of stress. The reasons for Constructive Living's effectiveness are clear.

Constructive Living is realistic and practical. No one is asserting that it is easy.

Brain Research Evidence

As Richard Restak, a neurologist, wrote in the Washington Post "we are what we do rather than what we think, fantasize or otherwise inwardly experience about ourselves...We are truly ourselves only when we act." He bases his assertion on recent brain research by Benjamin Libet at UCSF which indicates that subjects' brains show activity milliseconds before they become conscious of "choosing" to flex their forefingers. Moreover, the subjects can choose not to flex during the milliseconds between their awareness of their intention to move and the actual flexing. The ability to veto the brain's decision may be the locus of free will, according to Libet.

The theoretical implications for Constructive Living are worth considering. For decades Constructive Living action theory held that thoughts, feelings, and other mental events are natural phenomena, not completely under our conscious control. They are natural and spontaneous responses arising from our environments, histories, and so forth. Now we begin to see some neurophysiological evidence for the Constructive Living action assertion. The natural environment of our minds includes our brain activity. The brain responds naturally and spontaneously to the Reality that presents itself. Then the brain generates impulses that we interpret as thoughts, feelings, decisions, and the like.

Constructive Living theory holds that the locus of control in our lives lies in behavior. We define who we are by what we do. Accepting thoughts, feelings, moods, and other mental events is our only recourse; they aren't completely within our control; what else can we do but accept them? To struggle with the undefeatable is to play a losing game of life. Now there is scientific evidence supporting the theory generated from human experience. The control and freedom in our lives does come through what we do.

It is satisfying to find scientific support for Constructive Living principles. But scientific theory changes. Experimental refutations of Libet's procedures may appear in future reports. Our experience provides solid support for our understandings that mental events aren't totally controllable by our will and that within the domain of behavior lies personal freedom and control of our lives.

Searching for the Source

By now you are familiar with the notion that feelings are natural aspects of Reality. If we take the trouble to search, we can find a natural, understandable source for any feeling. One source of any anxious feeling, for example, is a strong desire. Anxiety about failing comes from a strong desire to succeed. Anxiety about meeting people comes from a strong desire to be liked and respected. The stronger the positive desire, the greater is the anxiety associated with it. The late Dr. Takehisa Kora, a Morita therapist in Tokyo, wrote on this subject in great detail. In Constructive Living we sometimes ask our students to look for the positive desire underlying their specific fears and worries. When they discover the underlying constructive desires they are better able to accept the naturalness of the anxieties, too.

But the search for the deep, hidden origins of our unpleasant feelings isn't always so important. Whether we discover the source or not, all feelings are natural results of our life situations. Recognize it or not, accept it or not, emotions are no more than another natural aspect of our life reality. We may survey our feelings, however, to discern whether they are pointing toward some necessary action.

The attitude of acceptance of feelings is much more important than the search for their deep origins. Acceptance puts emotions in proper perspective. They occur, we recognize them, and we go on about doing what it is necessary to do in our lives. In fact, the search for the deep sources of our feelings can falsely validate an importance they need not carry in our lives. The search can distract us from the constructive behaviors that lie right before our eyes. Haven't you met people who are so caught up in discovering the hidden sources of their distressing feelings that their lives appear to be at a standstill? They are so involved in introspection that their houses aren't clean and their offices are cluttered with work undone.

Creative artists, however, may find it useful to explore their feelings in detail in order to discover novelties worth expressing in their work. Lay people, too, may wish to explore their feelings for the sheer fascination of the intricacy to be found there, the connections with the rest of reality. Nevertheless, such a hobby must be kept in perspective and balanced with constructive, purposeful action. Failure to do so will inevitably lead to aimless wandering in the labyrinths of the mind, a selfish and ultimately unsatisfying preoccupation.

For most of us it is sufficient to accept the emotions that surface, check to see whether they suggest some necessary action (pain, for example, may tell us to get our hands off the hot stove), act appropriately to the circumstances, and get on about noticing and responding to other aspects of reality.

III. CONSTRUCTIVE LIVING AND THE MIND

Silence

It seems to me that people keep burying their thoughts under a deluge of information input. Many people turn on the radio in their car or at home or at work and leave it on as a sort of defense against listening to their own thoughts. What their own minds might churn up is for them frightening or uninteresting, without value. Television and novels serve the same purpose of distraction for some.

One of the privileges of being a writer is that long periods are spent quietly with one's own mind. A kind of intimacy develops in the silence. One learns the mind's foibles and strengths. One cannot develop such an intimacy with one's mind while watching television or conversing or playing football. Isolation and silence are necessary. Meditation offers such benefits; so do long private walks in the woods.

Getting to know ourselves in secluded surroundings in silence is a worthwhile endeavor. We discover facets that never turn up by the light of a video screen.

In our extended association with television, film, and radio we suffer from a distortion of time. We live vicariously through the characters of dramas and comedies. We suffer their pain and adopt their solutions to their adversities. We are exposed to a wide span of life problems and remedies, more than any other people at any other time. But these media-housed difficulties emerge and their resolutions take place within hours. We may come to expect rapid relief of our own life predicaments, too. The pace of our lives cannot accelerate to equal that of the media.

The fog softens the view from my Coos Bay window this morning. The greens gradually shift to grays and browns and white. By afternoon the fog bank will soundlessly recede over the ocean again, and damp leaves will glisten silver green. Just notice and appreciate what is there, and wait for the inevitable change. Dip into timelessness.

Tying Shoelaces as a Spiritual Practice

There are many ways to tie shoelaces--bow knots, double bow knots, square knots, granny knots, and so forth. The tying of the knot is a spiritual practice whatever knot is used. Whether the knot is tied mindfully or not, whether the knot is tied with recognition that the act is spiritual or not, the act is, nevertheless, spiritual. Every act is so. Nothing need be added to an act or incorporated into an act to make it spiritual. All acts are spiritual just as they are.

Reality cannot be divided conceptually into spiritual and non-spiritual categories to any useful end. It is all sacred. It is all holy. Reality is what it is. Recognize it or not. The cricket is chirping, the cars roar past the window.

Why, then, in Constructive Living do we encourage mindful, attentive action? If it isn't the mindfulness which makes an act holy, if any method of shoelace tying is a sacred act, why go to the trouble to tie shoes well, with full attention? The answer is simple: holy activities deserve to be recognized as such. We can ignore the pain that our births caused our mothers, but the pain existed nevertheless. We can thoughtlessly slam the car into gear or ease it gently into gear with grateful attention, but the car continues to serve us.

So if you walk inside an edifice and voices become hushed and faces show awe and reverence, those voices and faces show how carelessly their owners view the reality outside that edifice. Nowhere is holier than anywhere else. It is all holy--the shoelaces, the temples, the cricket, the cars--all of it.

Someone will surely say, "That's an admirable ideal, but humans aren't capable of seeing everything as holy. So we select some representative objects for veneration." It is true that we humans can't see the holiness in everything all the time. Yet we may have moments of seeing shoes and toilet seats and keys and cups as holy if they aren't excluded from that category by designated temples and crosses and altars.

Our eyes don't make reality holy, our actions don't make reality holy, it simply is that way. How reassuring! Because sometimes we forget.

Once I bought a hair dryer as a birthday gift for a friend on the very day her old hair dryer broke. The next day as I was riding a train I had a premonition that a nearby passenger would spill something on my slacks and she did. The Japanese call such occurrences "fushigi." That word can be translated as 'marvelous' or 'wondrous.' Our everyday lives are filled with marvelous events, but we take them for granted. Where do the fresh moments we experience come from? Where do our thoughts come from? Where do the words we speak come from? Where does the rich variety of reality come from? How is it that reality provides this particular chair for my comfort, this air conditioner, this word processor, these slippers? The vast efforts of others in our behalf are readily discovered with a little reflection, but they are nonetheless marvelous. It is this sense of wonder about ordinary life which characterizes the student of Constructive Living. As we have seen, there is no religious separation of life into the holy and mundane--sabbath and weekday, priest and layperson, worship and work, prayer and conversation, temple and house. It is all holy, if you wish to use such a term.

I want to put the mystery and transcendence back into our perception of everyday reality where it belongs. We can only see reality as "ordinary" by ignoring its magnificence. And so I resist making Constructive Living into a form of therapy, like Morita therapy and Naikan therapy. I want these Constructive Living ideas to be natural, normal parts of everyday life--not set apart as special techniques applicable only to neurotic, suffering people.

Religion, also, has too much become the domain of the "set apart." For the most part the institutionalized religions of our day have become talk shows with ministers and priests in hierarchies of talk show hosts. Religious practitioners talk too much about talking. Too little do they talk about experiencing their faith; too little do they ground their beliefs in everyday reality.

My second fundamental quarrel with organized religion has to do with its divisiveness. In the first place religion tends to divide the world into that which is holy or sacred and that which is ordinary, secular, mundane. Even in some Zen centers (center is a much preferable term to temple) where people should know better, there is an attitude of reverence and awe as members enter the zendo where zazen meditation takes place. That same attitude isn't exhibited when entering the dining room or cars or the toilet. That's a fundamental mistake fostered by religion. *All of reality* is worthy of our deep respect.

A similar divisiveness separates humans themselves into sacred and secular categories and into hierarchies within those categories. Certain roles are created that are set apart and (however it may be denied) set above other roles. These roles are signified by special titles (pope, bishop, D.Min., and dress-- often the colors of robes have hierarchical significance. Some religious leaders are served as though they alone were representatives of superior beings (God, Buddha, etc.).

Such religious pigeonholing promotes the notion that the sacred is to be approached in certain places at certain times through the good offices of certain chosen people. But the sacred is around you, is you, all the time, is time.

"Once, the Church understood this; there must be a perpetual mysticism, perpetual experience...'Pray without ceasing' means pray now, in the present moment." (p. 76, quoted from the journal of Father Sylvan in Needleman, 1980)

"What then is the Constructive Living attitude toward 'higher truths?'" you may ask. Unfortunately, should you present such a query I have no idea what you are asking. Which truths are higher than others? If you are talking about truths which cannot be tested by experience in ordinary reality then I suspect that you have no idea what you are asking. Robert Heinlein wrote similar views in *To Sail Beyond the Sunset*. Watch out for people who talk about untestable spiritual truths, he warned, they are after your money. And, "'Eventually I learned that the Church is run solely for the benefit of the priesthood, not for the good of our people.'" (p. 334) And, again, "'But you must respect another man's religious beliefs!' For Heaven's sake, why? Stupid is stupid--faith doesn't make it smart." (p. 373)

Having read all the above criticism, don't get the idea that I am against religion altogether. I simply oppose the thoughtless, automatic, self-serving religion which interferes with the genuine needs of humans to see beyond themselves. Both Morita and Yoshimoto recognized that their approaches brought serious students to the doorway of true religious experience, whatever form it might take for the individual. They were right. Constructive Living, based on their insights, offers the same opportunity.

Groom or Gloom

Appearance isn't everything, but it is something. Have you ever thought there was no need to shave or put on make-up one morning because no one was going to see you that day anyway? Have you ever failed to comb or brush your hair because you felt so miserable? Have you ever lounged around in robe and slippers well into the afternoon? I want to present here two different perspectives on why such practices are wrong; the perspectives come from the action and reciprocity aspects of Constructive Living.

You may have read the Constructive Living action maxim "Behavior wags the tail of feelings." In Constructive Living we point out that our actions influence how we think and feel. Because what we do is the most controllable aspect of our lives (even more controllable than thinking) we use our actions to provide the steady groundwork for building our lives. Although we may not feel like keeping ourselves well-groomed we can do it (within the limits of any physical handicaps we might have, of course). From this perspective, keeping ourselves spruced up is simply something that needs doing. It will have an effect on other features of our lives.

The issue of hypocrisy may arise here. Aren't we lying to others when we put on a good face even when feeling miserable or lazy? Isn't it better to be true to ourselves? Underlying these questions is the issue of untruth for personal gain at the expense of others. That sort of hypocrisy isn't what concerns us here. Grooming is just doing the best we can in a given situation. The fact of the matter is that we may find our feelings changing to fit our new face. Conversely, sloppy attire and an unwashed face may provoke more gloom.

Here is another perspective on maintaining a pleasant appearance--whatever the personal effect of keeping ourselves well groomed might be, the world deserves to see us looking our best. What you are about to read may appear strange, but I ask you to consider it with an open mind. Let's start with the most acceptable argument. Maybe your family members have seen you looking terrible before, and they love you anyway. But your family deserves to see you looking clean and unrumpled. Consider your appearance a sort of gift, an initial payment on a social loan from your loved ones, a loan you need to work at paying off. Taken a step further, there is chance that someone else might see you or telephone you--a delivery person, perhaps, or a neighbor. And your voice on the phone might be influenced by your attire and personal grooming. They went to the trouble to contact you; the least you can do is put your best face forward.

Again, this line of thought has nothing to do with the effects of a neat appearance on you, but it is about the effects of how you look on the world around you. Now comes the step that might seem odd. Even if no one has any direct contact with you at all that day the furniture and walls and magazines and dishes and washbasin and wastebasket and all those objects around you deserve to see you looking at your best. But they have no eyes! Right. And they are just things; they haven't earned any special treatment! Partly right; they are things. Whether they deserve special treatment depends on your point of view. It would be hard to argue that your washbasin and wastebasket haven't been useful to you in the past. It might be convenient to ignore their service just because they don't move around on their own and talk. It might be convenient to classify a large part of reality as "objects" which don't merit thoughtful recognition for service and so don't merit any return from us. Our debts are reduced quite simply that way, rather like the imaginative notion of doing away with the national debt by legally abolishing it.

Think about it. Whether you notice it or not, acknowledge it or not you are served daily by numerous people and things.

So we've considered this issue of grooming from a couple of angles. One way to check out the value of these suggestions is to verify them through experience. The investment is likely to be worth your while.

Broad minds

I never met a mind that didn't judge. That's what minds do-- they discriminate, evaluate. Everybody's mind does that. What makes some humans stand out from others is that they don't let their judging minds push their behavior around.

Rather than making efforts to eliminate mental judgments-- another of those useless struggles which focus needless attention on natural functions of the mind--simply note the judgments and get on with whatever is more important to be doing. By living constructively we outgrow such narrow-mindedness. Getting caught up in an obsession with perfecting the mind is itself a sort of narrow-mindedness. Such pursuits restrict one's openness to the supporting world, one's attention to what needs doing, one's awareness of new information.

Narrow-minded people don't make broad theories or think grand thoughts. They try to keep their minds under control by means of one-pattern thinking. How dull! The mind should flow naturally and free while their behavior remains under rein.

One of the ways the mind tries to expand is by gathering information. Gathering information seems a basic goal of humans. We travel to get information about others' customs and environments; we watch news on television; we open the envelopes of ads even when we know we're not going to buy the products; we attend adult education classes. We are information gatherers and sorters and evaluators. Our minds just aren't satisfied without new information and new problems with which to work.

Something in our minds causes us to search for reality, for truth. We are fascinated by accidents, by disasters--even by those aspects of reality which are disgusting or horrifying. We are drawn to reality even when it is unpleasant and painful--we want to know, for example, when we have cancer or when we are not expected to live much longer. This push to know reality underlies both our search within religion and our research within science. It prompts us to read newspapers and magazines, to watch television and to telephone distant friends.

Even when our sources of information about reality are patently unreliable or untrustworthy or deliberately biased we still want to know the reality of that false information. How strong is our desire to know about the way things are!

Minds seek challenges, too. I sometimes wonder whether the alcohol problem in middle-class and upper-middle-class men and women is less tied to the meaningless of life as it is to the ease of life. When life produces few challenges, when daily routine is relatively easily mastered, our minds may generate problems. Can I drink and still carry out my life? Can I get away with this vice without its consuming me? Maybe others can't, but I can meet this challenge. If this hunch has some merit, then it is important to offer alternate stimuli, hurdles, to people with alcohol abuse problems. The mental exercise involved in living life with full attention may be just what is needed.

It is noteworthy that people with a lot of neurotic moments seem to be obsessed with internally generated information. They focus primarily on distressing data about their own feelings. They notice their feeling centeredness and then judge or criticize themselves for being feeling-centered. Then they feel even worse. It may take some time for them to realize that feeling is all right, noticing is all right, judging is all right, criticizing is all right, and even feeling worse is all right. What is not all right is letting these natural functions of the mind get in the way of doing the positive, constructive behaviors which will change the focus of their natural minds.

It may be narrow-minded to attempt to construct a life philosophy out of thinking on the subject. A life philosophy is the product of one's life, not the other way around. We don't choose a lifeway and then live by it. We grow a life philosophy over years of living one. Excessive rumination about life purpose may be a distraction from what needs doing right before our noses. There is a time for discovering purpose and a time for planning activities, but then there is a time to move on to the next immediate task.

Flip flop goes the lazy mind. People with lazy minds don't recognize the limits of their minds. Then they encounter some information which tells them they are limited by their thinking. Immediately they turn completely about and think that there are no barriers except in their minds. Similarly, when they discover that they are capable of doing something previously thought impossible they begin to think they can do anything at all. They think that Constructive Living is Japanese or it's not. They suspect that Constructive Living must be psychotherapy or not. They hold that this constructive lifeway is helpful to everyone or it's not helpful to anyone. In lazy moments our minds try to play either-or games of opposition because to do so is easier than to look at scales of gray percentages. Oversimplification through opposition is a tendency we all need to combat in order to achieve more moments of broad-minded thinking.

People whose broad-minded mental products stand out from those of their peers intrigue us. How amazing is the variety of human mental activity! I sometimes feel an affinity to iconoclasts--to Bankei, the rebel Zen Master of the 17th Century, for example. Iconoclasts don't make themselves. They are just doing their best to describe the world as it looks to them. The eyes of those around them produce iconoclasts.

Reading can provide a mind-broadening exercise. For example, science fiction can be important by allowing us to see humanity from a distance or from an alien or universal point of view. It is not we Americans or we Japanese, but we humans, we inhabitants of this planet. Well-written science fiction stretches and broadens the mind.

The Working Mind

Generating ideas

Minds process information. That's what minds do. When there is no information to process the mind invents information through a function we call imagination.

A middle-aged lady found herself back in social circulation. She put on make-up, fixed her hair, dressed appropriately, then worried about what might happen at the party that night. What if? Would he? Might they? Her mind was generating scenarios to work on. In a few hours reality would give her mind real data to work on. In the meantime her mind needed something to do. She didn't know about keeping it busy with real information while waiting for her escort to pick her up.

Put yourself in a quiet room long enough and your mind will generate sounds. Put yourself in a dark room and, in time, you will see things. Put a stationary light in that dark room and your mind will imagine the light is moving. The mind seeks information and will generate it when enough isn't forthcoming from reality.

When we don't want to be carried away with imagining we can assure a flow of reality-based information through proper behavior and attention to attention. Moving our bodies increases the likelihood of inputting information from reality--a stroll through our neighborhood or a park, a vacation, volunteer work, attending evening classes. Isolating ourselves provides fruitful opportunities for imagination to work. When I write, for example, it is best for me to be alone in a quiet room. But, in general, when we want less imagining, it is helpful to be interacting with other people. Being around others won't eliminate the function of imagination, but it will give it some realistic information to work on.

We can notice our habits of daydreaming and our tendencies to worry about illusory incidents. We have some control over bringing our attention back to our immediate surroundings. Physical activity seems to help. It is helpful to outline and underline passages in a book in order to keep our attention fully on the contents. It is easier still to refinish an antique chair than to read. And so forth. There is something about physical activity that facilitates pulling our attention to reality and away from imagination.

As I walk through the forest my mind seeks the variety that Nature provides. Then it looks for the orderliness of pattern. My mind needs both variety and order. I suspect that yours does, too. Reality provides both variety and order, so does imagination.

Generating preoccupations

Toraware is a Japanese word for non-acceptance, a kind of artificial attachment to one aspect of reality and a concomitant rejection of other elements of natural reality. The late Yozo Hasegawa, a leader in the Morita mental health movement in Japan, made a theoretical contribution to the understanding of *toraware* which moved it out of the narrow psychiatric concern for obsession with neurotic symptoms into the broader realm of obsession with work or love or even preoccupation with therapeutic ideas. In other words, we can be obsessed not only with hand washing or avoiding heights, but also with getting ahead at work, with finding a marriage partner, with self improvement.

Toraware means literally "to be caught by something" in Japanese. *Toraware* narrows the spotlight of the mind to some aspect of life and shuts out other aspects. It is contrasted with the open acceptance of reality and the flowing mind which moves naturally to attend to a variety of stimuli. The opposite of *toraware* is acceptance and non-attachment. *Toraware* results from applying some artificial mental construct to what is, and then being more attracted to the construct than to reality. It is a sort of mental clouding of one's vision of reality.

We live in a complex world. There are many possible goals for us, many ways to act to achieve those goals. We are pulled by all sorts of voices from about us and within us. To more-or-less single-mindedly focus in on a single goal or class of goals gives direction to our living, even when that direction is destructive. Few people seem to notice that one of the allures of drugs is the single-minded devotion to securing them. If the addict can just get the next fix, that is sufficient in life. Contrast that goal with the middle-aged businessman aiming to pay off debts, buy a new car, please his wife, understand his children, keep from getting too flabby, and so forth. Life simplified down to a single goal has its attractiveness, even when that goal is negative and narrow.

Considering the frequency with which paranoia is encountered in normal and mentally-disordered people there is relatively little written about this form of suffering. The delusion that someone else is plotting to do one harm can be found to some degree in everyone at one time or another. The boundary between paranoia and a realistic appraisal of our enemies' interests may be unclear at times. The thesis here is simply that obsessions with drugs (including alcohol), sex, money, love, paranoia and the like are foci for simplifying the organization of stimulus input from the world and providing a limited set of goals from the spectrum of goals reality offers us. In other words, drugs, sex, money, love and paranoia serve to help some people focus their attention on a limited set of information from their sensory input, to make clear (though possibly incorrect) sense of that information, and to limit the range of relevant goals.

Just as the lover "reads into" the loved one's acts gestures of concern and affection, so the paranoid individual sees threat in others' behavior. All the world loves a lover, we say. The lover throws the net of simplification widely, seeing affection and tolerance in everyone. Similarly, the paranoid person expands the strategy for understanding a particular foe to encompass everyone around. We need not posit a psychological mechanism of projection here. The lover does not attribute his own love to others. His love is quite different from that which he supposes others to possess.

Obsession with money, fame, food, whatever, acts to simplify the decision-making process in a complicated world. Obsession "boils down" reality to a rigid, bit-sized chunk...unfortunately, it is a chunk that is no longer reality.

Morita noticed that when neurotics in Japan said "I shouldn't feel nervous" they implied "I need more will power to control my feelings; I lack character and moral fiber for feeling this way." Our American neurotics also say "I shouldn't feel nervous." But behind the Westerners' words are the thoughts "I don't have my life together; I need a better background or a better therapy." The Japanese people of Morita's day in their neurotic moments tended to see the flaws in themselves. The American people in neurotic moments tend to see the flaws in their upbringing, their circumstances, their lack of appropriate social or psychotherapeutic support. As Western influence expands in Japan modern Japanese people tend to move toward blaming their personal problems on others--schoolmates, parents, workmates, society, and so forth. Both Japanese and Americans, however, see the anxiety or fear or obsession as the undesirable outcome of some sort of flaw, personal and/or social. Neither Japanese nor American is likely to see the anxiety or fear or obsession as natural, with both positive and negative aspects. And, from a larger perspective, both Japanese and Americans are likely to be preoccupied (obsessed, caught) in trying to cure (overcome, fix) their neurotic suffering.

Immediate Cure

Eliminating the dualism of means and end
The possibility of "cure" for neurosis is already present in every suffering person's mind. Constructive living need not be considered a means of achieving freedom from neurotic suffering sometime in the future. It is not merely a method to be used to rid ourselves of unnecessary misery "ultimately." It is about being cured now, in this moment. Living constructively right now is already cure. The means and the end are the same.

My concern for my students is less in their someday becoming well than in their being well immediately.

There is an interesting parallel here with one of the ideas of Dogen, the famous Zen master. Dogen (1200-1253) denied that sitting in Zen meditation was a means that one could practice to achieve future enlightenment. He argued that sitting in zazen meditation was itself enlightenment. He saw no dualistic split between practicing and achieving this end result.

It is the very same in Constructive Living. In those moments when we lose ourselves in a constructive activity, our neurotic suffering is gone. My students may undertake an assigned exercise with the intent of working toward personal growth or "cure." However, when they are caught up in composing their assigned letter of apology and gratitude, when they are engrossed in cleaning out the kitchen cabinet, they are no different from anyone whom they would hesitate to call neurotic. In those moments they are free from neurotic suffering. Instant cure. Instant satori.

Such freedom isn't trivial. It is the accumulation of moment after moment of constructive behavior that allows us to call ourselves normal. It is this doing that is the distraction from our self-centered merry-go-round of pain. The means is also the end.

Eliminating the dualism of mind and body.

Constructive Living is not a way of training the mind. It is a way of using the bodymind. The doing of a task at hand is not merely an action of the body. It is an action of the bodymind. Morita called this principle *shinshin doitsu* (literally, "mind-body same").

Psychology in the West pays lip service to psychosomatic principles, but when we look at Western psychotherapy, we see practices that focus almost entirely on changing mental processes. Yet the physical movement of the body is both a reflection of and a lever for changing the mind. The last sentence is imprecise from our point of view because it makes it appear that changed behavior occurs and then the mind changes. More accurately, changed behavior is already changed mind, and changed mind is already changed behavior. The two are different ways of talking about the same set of phenomena. When was the last time you saw a mind? The concept of "mind" is built on inferences from bodily behavior. An alteration in one is an alteration in the other.

Again, we find an interesting parallel from Buddhism in the notion of *sokushin Jobutsu* or "enlightenment with this very body." Kukai, the founder of Shingon Buddhism, saw that it makes no sense to talk about the enlightenment of the mind alone or the achievement of some mental Nirvana in the future. The bodymind must participate in any insight or wisdom.

Eliminating the duality of subjective/objective

There is a famous quote from the Chinese Zen master Ch'ing-yuan

(1067-1120): "Before I had studied Zen for thirty years, I saw mountains as mountains and waters as waters. When I arrived at a more intimate knowledge, I came to the point where I saw that mountains are not mountains and waters are not waters. But now that I have got the very substance I am at rest. For it is just that I see mountains once again as mountains, and waters once again as waters."

I am much indebted to William LaFleur, whose book, The Karma of Words, so clearly spells out the Buddhist concepts for which I find these parallels in Constructive Living action thought and practice. LaFleur writes with regard to the above quote:

"It might he said that in Buddhism the problem posed by the symbolizing process of the mind is not unlike that posed by the habitual daydreams, fantasies, and projections that disturb our capacity for 'right seeing.' In a sense, the symbolizing process is itself a digression, a move away from the clear recognition of mountains as merely mountains, waters as merely waters."

Neurotic thinking is filled with the symbolizing that interferes with our seeing what reality presents to us. For example, when anthropophobic people are about to be introduced to someone at a social gathering, their minds are filled with all sorts of symbol baggage. There are memories of past introduction experiences that were embarrassing or anxiety-filled, there are desires to be liked and respected, there are fears of what the other person will be thinking of them, worries about appearance, and so forth. The reality of the person they are about to meet--the face, the clothing, the name, the interests, and words of that person--are likely to be missed because of all the symbolic interference with reality. The mountain is no longer a mountain. It has become a fearful challenge. In Constructive Living we aim at being realistic. Of course, no one views reality with total objectivity. We all carry some symbols and selective attention in our encounters with the world before our eyes. But it turns out that as we accumulate constructive life experiences, the mountains look more like mountains and the waters look more like waters.

Eliminating the dichotomy of good/bad

In our approach to Constructive Living we recognize that all people have some neurotic characteristics in some moments and all neurotic people have nonneurotic characteristics in some moments. We refuse to view humans in polar categories of normal and neurotic. Each conceptual category contains the other. Tamura Yoshiro pointed out that early Tendai Buddhists in Japan had already discovered that good and evil interpenetrate. These extreme values aren't mutually exclusive; instead, they interpenetrate.

Changing from a primarily neurotic to a generally constructive lifestyle isn't just desirable; it is also terrifying. The Zen master Rinzai wrote that the ordinary person is terrified of transmigration. We are all afraid of extreme change, uncertainty, death, fate, and "getting well." We often choose the familiarity of boredom and suffering rather than the uncertainty of change. What I define as a good or positive change for you may be negative from your perspective.

"The True Man of the Way. . . accepts things as they come. When he wants to walk he walks, when he wants to sit he sits; he never has a thought of seeking Buddhahood." Rinzai's words are often quoted. In the same vein, the graduate of the constructive lifeway accepts reality as it comes. When he finds it purposeful to walk, he walks; when he finds it useful to sit, he sits; he never has a thought of seeking (or checking on the progress of) his cure. The parallels are apparent.

From the preceding examples we can see that the absoluteness of good and bad is lost in the flux of changing circumstance. Is it good to be "normal"? But "normal" contains neurotic moments, too. Is it good to become "cured"? But cure is painful and terrifying. Is it good to walk? to sit? That depends upon the situation, the conditions, what needs to be done. Rather than spending a lot of time and effort trying to come up with an invulnerable structure of absolute good and bad, we choose to approach reality circumstantially, asking concretely what needs to be done in this moment. To be sure, we take into account the likely effects of our actions on others and on ourselves. But philosophical speculation about ideals too easily becomes a distraction from engaging in what needs doing right now.

Working within the flux

In Constructive Living we emphasize the changeableness of feelings. A parallel Buddhist psychological principle is *mujo*, "all is flux." Everything is always changing. Perhaps so, yet even the Zen monk in training finds that doing what needs to be done provides some stability and order and purposeful direction in this ever changing world. The monk may find that what needs to be done is sitting meditation, sweeping, mopping, chanting, eating in a particular fashion, and so forth.

We, too, create some stability, order, and direction through purposeful behavior. Despite the flux of feelings and headtripping we can reach the haven of disciplined behavior. We have come full circle to the beginning passage on the equivalence of means and ends. The order and stability exist as we create them by our doing. As you read these words, you are already changed. That is, the quality of your attentive reading is already important change, whatever the value of the content of this essay. What you are doing now isn't "preparing" you for self-improvement. It either is self-improvement or it is not. The quality of the doing is vital.

Scenes

When my clients talk about the events of the past week, they tend to talk in terms of scenes or episodes. These scenes have clear beginnings and endings. I find myself listening to a brief tale organized like a television story. I believe that my clients have been influenced by television and other media to carve up their experience into scenes. I often need to ask, "What did you do next?" I want to know what my student did after what he or she thought was the end of the scene.

Let me offer an example. Clyde tells me of the scene in which he embarrassed himself before his fellow cooking-school classmates by raising his hand to ask a question. Then when called upon, he forgot what he wanted to ask. He finishes by telling me he felt like crawling into a hole to escape their eyes. As far as Clyde was concerned, the scene ended there.

"What did you do next?" I ask.

"What do you mean?"

"I want to know what you did right after that, while you were feeling embarrassed."

"Well, the teacher went on with his lecture, so I grabbed my pen and started taking notes again."

Clyde had come a long way from the days in which embarrassment was followed by hours of self-recrimination and even absences from school. If he had chosen to end his "scene" a bit later, he would have turned out to be a hero instead of a goat. The forgetting was not controllable directly by his will. With his best effort he couldn't come up with the question that caused him to raise his hand. But what he did while feeling embarrassed was another opportunity for success (in this case, taking notes). And Clyde succeeded.

Life doesn't present itself in episodes or scenes. It is a continuous flow of opportunities, failures, successes, punctuated only by periods of sleep--and sometimes then, too, we experience the flow of dreams. When failure looms (or when success lies within reach), the important question to be asking continues to be, "What has reality brought that needs to be done?" Then, what did you do next?

Purposeful Living

A few years ago I met a man, Mr. Lewin, with a great dream and great energy. The dream itself was quite properly grand and worthy. What bothered me was that there was too much Lewin in Lewin's dream. It seemed that his fine purpose was confused with another, less significant one, impressing others with his importance. It is important to be clear about our purposes. I must be careful about my purpose in writing this book, too. I want you to finish reading it with a fair sense of what Constructive Living is about. So I mix the theoretical with the personal and practical contents in order to avoid a presentation about the ideal as opposed to the real.

Throughout human history people have wondered about purposeful living, and there has been no lack of teachers to advise them about it: Plato, Confucius, Billy Graham, Dogen Zenji, Mao Tse-tung, Voltaire, and Norman Vincent Peale, to name just a few. However, there have been scores of lesser-known advisers in every age. In our era one large category of life guides are called psychotherapists. For all the use of medical jargon about mental illness, symptoms, diagnoses, and cures, therapists teach their "patients" or "clients" a lifeway either explicitly or implicitly, either by direction or by model. There is an insightful book written by Perry London many years ago titled *The Modes and Morals of Psychotherapy*. In it

London points out that every psychotherapeutic system contains a set of values, a definition of what it is to be fully human, and notions about suffering and the resolution of suffering. Psychotherapists, too, have purposes.

The purposes of Constructive Living are quite clear. They are, again, to teach students to accept feelings as they are, to know their purposes, and to do what needs to be done. All the other techniques of Constructive Living's action aspect are aimed at achieving these purposes or goals. For example, I may ask clients to report on the contents of their closets, or to describe the persons that they passed as they walked or drove to the teaching session, or to indicate where the fire exits are in buildings they have recently entered. These exercises help them to develop skills of observation. Observation helps us to be aware of what reality is bringing us to do in each moment. How can we be aware of what needs doing when we aren't paying attention to our circumstances? More advanced students not only notice their surroundings but begin to notice themselves as part of the surroundings and, ultimately, just to "notice." But that result goes beyond the more modest goals of acceptance, purpose, and action.

Another technique of Constructive Living utilizes physical activity to accomplish tasks when we feel overwhelmed by feelings. You may have noticed that when you are upset it is more difficult to balance a checkbook and study a text than it is to wash your car or rearrange furniture or do the vacuuming. While we wait for our feelings to settle down, we need not turn off our lives; we can continue with constructive activity, getting done what needs doing. Somehow it's easier to keep our minds on tasks that require physical effort. A reminder: the purpose of doing a task is to get the task done (to get the dishes clean, to clear the weeds from the garden, to dust the bookcase), and not to distract ourselves from unpleasant feelings (although that may be a beneficial side effect).

Performing physical action as an aid to concentration is as useful for mental work like bookkeeping and studying as it is for sweeping and gardening. When we underline, write out our thoughts on paper, outline the material we have read, or organize our desktop, we are likely to find it easier to attend to the mental task at hand. The more body movement aimed at achieving our goal, the better (even the movement of hand holding pen moving across paper can be helpful). The opposite approach, trying to keep every important point in mind, while merely exerting the will to keep the mind on a task, turns out to be less effective. For my office I have built a wooden podium that looks rather like a music stand. When I am tired from sitting in front of the computer, reading in the easy chair, or writing at the desk, I can stand and read at the podium, resting a book on it. Along the same lines, I sometimes conduct part of a teaching hour standing or walking alongside a student, especially when one or both of us is sleepy. Whatever our feelings (sleepiness, fatigue, rage, despair, fear), they need not distract us from purposeful behavior. And the behavior itself seems to pull us along toward our goals.

Constructive Living instructors emphasize that it is important to find suitable constructive purposes and hold to them, thus guiding behavior in a positive direction. The other side of that coin is that all behavior, positive or negative, is purposeful. Whatever you do there is an aim to it, a goal toward which the behavior is directed. The goal may be destructive or constructive or mixed. For example, the shy person may avoid social gatherings in order to prevent the feelings of inadequacy and loneliness that he feels in such situations. In a sense Constructive Living instruction asks the client to select constructive purposes and positive ways of achieving them instead of the already purposeful, but unconstructive behavior. Finding the purpose behind unconstructive behavior can be a useful undertaking because sometimes the original purpose can also be fulfilled in a positive way.

It is not a new idea that difficulties in life generate the construction of purpose. Continuous happiness, peace, and a life of ease would destroy us. Without anxiety and trouble, we could not survive. Without conflict and struggle, life would not choose to continue. It is not that suffering is good; it is necessary for our existence. To say this is not to say that all pain must be passively accepted. We are responsible for doing battle with the ills that plague us and others. Yet, if we were ever to succeed in eliminating all discontent, our human species would be doomed. We struggle, and in that struggle lies life's meaning. We are born fighters; we will find something to oppose. If we cannot find a worthy foe, we create one, even if that foe is ourselves. When our last enemy is vanquished, we shall die as individuals, as a species.

So don't seek anxiety-free living; don't strive for constant bliss. choose rather to continue your struggle. Resolve to react forcefully to the challenges of reality. Hold to your goals. Fight your fight. And live with purpose.

Remaking the Past

We are continuously creating our histories. What I do now will be filed away in tomorrow's past. Once this now has become part of my past it cannot be changed. Its successes cannot be taken away from me; its excesses cannot be erased. Constructive Living works to create a past that is filled with purposeful, meaningful activity. With such a past I become one-who-lives-constructively.

For it is our history that determines who we are now. I evaluate myself in terms of what has been my history. If I am one who ran away from troubles in the past then I see myself as a coward; if I am one who sacrificed for my principles then I am a principled person. Fortunately, we have the ability to create a new past by means of changing what we are doing now. This moment becomes the recent past. Then it begins to sink beneath the weight of even more recent events, like sediment on the floor of the ocean. The old floor of my past can be completely covered by layers of new behaviors and habits.

It is important to emphasize that the past doesn't determine what we do now. Rather, we determine what the past will become by what we do now. The way I handle a problem now need have no relationship with the way I handled a similar problem in the past. I can change who I am by trying new solutions to recurring problems, by tucking old behaviors safely into the past.

Helping Out

*"One morning Joshu was walking in front of the Zen Hall,
treading on the deep-drifted snow. He accidentally lost his
footing and fell in the snow. He cried out loudly, 'Help me out!
Help me out!' A monk heard him crying, came running, raising
clouds, and instead of helping the Master out of the snow, 'threw
himself in the snow too.' That is, the monk laid himself down in
the snow like the Master. Joshu, who could very well have given
the monk a blow of his stick, quite calmly returned to his room.*

"Now, did this monk help the old teacher out or not?"
(Shibayama, 1970, p. 226)

Sometimes there is nothing we can do to take away the
difficulty that is troubling someone we care about. They may be
dying or suffering because someone close to them has died.
They may have put themselves in trouble or danger, a situation
that we cannot salvage for them. No matter how strong our
desire to help we may be unable to change the distressing
circumstances.

At such times we may decide to throw ourselves into the
snow alongside our friend. We may choose to share some of the
misery and physical discomfort, to talk about the loss, to
empathize, to donate our time and our existence in order to be
with our grieving friend. Our efforts may not solve the problem;
they may not even relieve much of our friend's pain. But it is a
fine human gesture to dive into the snow anyway. It may be the
best we can do. For the friend. For us.   Contrast the effort of

diving into the snow with the indifference described by the novelist, Natsume Soseki:

"*Daisuke* has yet to meet the individual who, as he stood groaning beneath the oppression of Occidental civilization in the seething arena of the struggle for survival, was still able to shed genuine tears for another." (Soseki, 1978, p. 102)

Soseki was a perceptive critic of the dangers that accompanied the benefits of Western civilization as Japan adopted Western ways around the turn of this century. Competition in the economic sphere can spill over into a self-centered indifference to others' dilemmas in other areas of life. Especially in this modern era of an unseemly faith in economic measures of importance we must beware the danger of losing compassion. To dive into the snow is "doing compassion."

Some of the places in the modern world where I have seen compassion done are terminal care units in hospitals. I have spent time with dying people and those who care for them in Japan and in the United States. There seems to be a kind of humanization of the participants in some of those settings. Here I would like to consider some of the qualities that compose this humanization.

In these settings gifts are given frequently. The gifts are usually inexpensive, personal, and sometimes handmade. Among nurses, aides, patients, families and doctors, and within some of these groups small gifts are tokens of human worth--exchanged appreciation, treasured mementos, spots of bright color in pastel medical surroundings.

People listen more and better in these settings. They show special consideration for others. They give time above that required by their shifts to lend an ear.

People use time well, purposefully. It may appear that they are "merely" sitting and chatting, but they have given thought to the value of such activities. They know how important it is to invest time in those they care for and care about.

Some social conventions are waived or postponed. Conversations get down to business quicker. People speak more openly and straightforwardly about their desires, frustrations, worries, joys. You see the same tendency in some elderly married couples. They trust each other to hear what is really being said.

In terminal care units there is a sense of camaraderie among staff, and less of a status gap between patients and staff. People know each others' names. They know of the names of visitors as well as those who are about to die.

The needs of caregivers in such settings (medical staff, nursing staff, aides, and office personnel) should not be ignored. They are living/dying just as the patients are, though the slope of their demise may be more gradual. Each new moment is a birth, and each past moment is a death for them, for all of us.

IV. NEUROTIC SUFFERING

No Solution to a Pseudo Problem

Neurosis is as natural as living. Because we live we have desires and hopes. Because we have desires and hopes we have fears of failing to achieve them in the future and memories of having failed to achieve them in the past.

How can we handle these anticipatory fears and discouraging memories? How can we cope with the reality that our desires and dreams always extend beyond our abilities to attain them? One coping strategy is to try to pound down the desires to fit our capabilities, to try to achieve some merging of what we want with what we can have. That strategy appears attractive, but it is impossible to carry out successfully. It inevitably involves lying to ourselves about what we desire. Life *always* implies desires that exceed realistic limits.

Another coping strategy is to try to extend our capabilities to match our desires. Diligent study and hard work and striving for success may bring some rewards, but the desires keep growing apace, too. They always outstrip our efforts to attain complete satisfaction. So, this coping strategy, too, is impossible to carry out successfully. Though there is nothing wrong with making efforts to grow, learn, advance, succeed, we'll never achieve all we desire.

Neurotic misery is being caught by this discrepancy between what is desired and what is possible. Neurosis involves a misdirection of attention toward this inherently insoluble problem of life. Neurotic suffering is misdirected effort to resolve an unresolvable dilemma. No amount of effort works satisfactorily; no direct approach to the problem succeeds. The neurotic struggle produces frustration and a turning inward to the feelings that accompany the struggle. Perhaps at least we can eliminate somehow the feelings of anxiety about future desires being unsatisfied and the self doubts and self recriminations over past failures. But, no. There, too, we hit the dead end of impossibility.

Neither the basic problem of the discrepancy between desires and capabilities nor the sub-problem of the unpleasant feelings accompanying recognition of this discrepancy can be solved. What is there to do?

The remarkable key which allows us to escape from this dark closet of frustration is to give up on trying to solve the dilemma altogether. In other words, we recognize the discrepancy between what we want and who we are (what we can achieve) and accept it. We recognize the feelings of anxiety and inadequacy that come with living and accept them. There is no need to fight, no need to wish life were otherwise than it is. We are just fine as we are.

Once (not really once, but over and over again) we recognize the naturalness of this reality of discrepancy we can get on about directing our attention and efforts toward doing what is possible. We can begin to live constructively and realistically within the limits and potentials that life offers us. There has been no problem all along except for the one we created in our minds. There is only a naturally expansive set of desires, a naturally limited set of abilities to achieve them, and a pressure to achieve them all anyway.

To be alive is to need, to succeed and to fail, to be sometimes anxious and sometimes confident, sometimes regretful and sometimes satisfied. Life is just fine like that.

Wishing life were otherwise is to step back into the dark confines of the pseudo problem with no solution. Accepting life as it is allows freedom to work on *real* problems and to find *real* solutions.

Deciding to Decide to Decide

When one looks below the surface symptoms, the typical neurotic person found in Japan and most commonly treated by Constructive Living isn't particularly different from the sort of neurotic person we see in the United States. Toru Abe, a leading Morita therapist, described the characteristics of the Japanese *shinkeishitsu* neurotic person. I find it useful to read his description to my new patients in the United States. It helps them to realize that they are not alone in their misery, that their tendencies are shared even by members of another culture.

Abe notes that these neurotics tend to be persistent. On the one hand, their persistence is a positive trait in that they can stick to a situation in an attempt to finish it or get through it. On the other hand, the persistence may appear as an obsession; they do not let go of an idea or course of action, even when it is no longer useful. These neurotic people tend to be affected physiologically whenever there are changes or stresses in their lives. Headaches, insomnia, upset stomach, diarrhea, heart palpitations, loss of appetite, general weakness, and lethargy characterize their bodies' response to pressures from their environment.

They often have self-doubts. Is this course of action all right? Did I do it properly? What do others think of me? Such concerns are common with adolescents, but in their neurotic moments adults tend to spend more time thinking about such things, worrying about them. They find themselves unsatisfied even when reassured that they are doing quite well. As they grow older, their perfectionistic and idealistic inclinations continue. They demand more than one hundred percent from themselves and from others, too. This makes relations with others difficult. Not only do they criticize themselves for failing to live up to their own standards, they demand perfection from others, as well.

Abe further observes that these neurotic people are disposed to all-or-nothing thinking. They don't want to undertake something unless they are absolutely confident that they can accomplish it. Sometimes they stop a project in midstream because they discover that it is more difficult than they had believed at first. When they ask for advice, they want a clear choice: either A or B. They don't like the muddied gray areas of life.

Abe, like Fritz Perls (the founder of Gestalt Therapy), noted that neurotic people are self-protective. Much of what they do can be understood in terms of their efforts to avoid pain. These attempts to escape from ordinary discomfort lead them into further trouble and further dissatisfaction with their lives. As they move into middle age, the symptoms may shift from obsessions and phobias to anxiety neuroses. Anxiety neuroses generally revolve around the fear of death or loss of ordinary consciousness. Heart palpitations cause the person to fear a heart attack, dizziness provokes ruminations about a potential stroke. These anxiety "attacks" seem to appear out of nowhere, with no obvious precipitating circumstance. Some of my students have them most often just before bedtime.

Something that I have noticed about neurotic people in both the United States and Japan is that they try to turn nearly every action into a decision. They make nearly every act a psychological dilemma. The reality is that nothing is getting done except deciding. They are really deciding to decide, not deciding to act. By this process they push themselves away from reality-oriented behavior into a sort of paralysis within their own minds.

Neurotic people of this sort tend to be rather bright, rarely stupid. They may have strange impulses and random thoughts about leaping down the stairs or stripping themselves in front of a crowd, but they're not the kind of people who actually *do* crazy and wild or hurtful and malicious things. For all their fantasies and worries, they behave pretty conservatively. For the most part, I can trust my students' judgment about what needs to be done. Until they demonstrate otherwise, I assume that they are competent.

It isn't necessary to trust your own judgment, but if you act on it and events work out all right most of the time, then just continue to stumble along like the rest of us, without confidence some of the time, but doing what needs doing nevertheless.

From the Constructive Living perspective, there are really no neurotic people. We all have neurotic moments. Some people have more neurotic moments than others.

Successful Fools

The Japanese psychiatrist Morita wrote, "While considering that there is something wrong with your mind, while feeling pessimistic about yourself, just keep working your mind vigorously." Here is a viable alternative to the strange Western advice to try to make yourself feel confident and successful when you don't and you're not.

Can you see the reasonable nature of this approach? You don't need to try to convince yourself that you are fine and that all is well in your life or your mind. It's quite all right to recognize your failures and limitations and anxieties and obsessions, and even to feel hopeless and pessimistic about them. After all, that *is* the way you feel about them sometimes. But Morita's advice doesn't stop with merely accepting the reality that we can't run away from anyway. He advises us to keep on working those imperfect, distressed minds vigorously. By working our minds vigorously he means to keep noticing what Reality sends our way and to attend carefully to doing well those moment-by-moment activities of which our lives are composed. Feel despair but take out the trash. Be pessimistic but plan your vacation. While feeling depressed shave. Walk the depths of hopelessness but prepare and show up for the job interview. While berating yourself for this morning's mistake don't miss the freeway turnoff.

It is quite all right to be the fool who lives life well.

Mirrors

I remember as a child sitting on the padded board laid across the arms of a sturdy metal barber's chair. I could see my face reflected in the mirror, and the reflection of the reflection, and the reflection of the reflection of the reflection. Each reflection bouncing off the mirrors in front and behind distorted the image ever so slightly until it dipped out of sight.

Neurosis is rather like watching reflections in barber shop mirrors. There is nothing really wrong with my clients just as they are. But they are obsessed with their distorted views of themselves. As the Zen people would put it, they already are Buddhas; they don't need some special enlightenment. But they don't recognize who they are and what they have already. So they come for "guidance" or "training" or "coaching" to be relieved of their suffering.

In their reflected images they see themselves as hurting more than other people, interfering with and interfered with in their movement toward success and happiness. They are unnecessarily miserable, but the fault lies not in themselves, and not even in their upbringing or in more recent tragedies. The problem lies in the images they create, images of how life ought to be, what might have been, who they should be instead of who they are.

If they insist on being obsessed with reflections I advise them to follow the infinity of reflections wholeheartedly until they become tired of the progressive distortion. For example, if they criticize themselves, I ask them to criticize their criticisms of themselves, and then to criticize themselves criticizing their self criticism. Why do they have confidence in their self-doubts? Why not doubt their self-doubts? And doubt themselves doubting their doubts about themselves? And so on. There is merit in lacking confidence in their own lack of confidence. My students simply aren't neurotic enough. They follow the images partway and then stop, believing them. To follow the reflections on and on reveals their absurd distortions.

The reality of me is just me.

Changing Who We Are

Years ago I spoke to a group of patients and ex-patients at a local Veterans Administration psychiatric hospital. One patient would soon be discharged; he was anticipating a return to the same stressful family environment in which he had been living when he was admitted to the hospital. He asked for suggestions about minimizing the negative effects of this situation after he returned home. He also wanted to know what to do about the anxiety he felt about leaving the hospital.

There are many parallels to this young man's dilemma in our lives. There are uncomfortable settings and upsetting people we must return to again and again--perhaps at work or at home or in an apartment building or neighborhood or among in-laws. We dread facing them. In a similar way, we hesitate to leave the familiar and comfortable for the unknown. A mental hospital places limits on a patient's rights and freedom, but it soon becomes a place of familiarity and security. Patients make friends with other patients and with staff members. Returning to the lonely, competitive world outside the hospital becomes a frightening step into possible failure.

The constructive advice we can offer a fellow human facing these conditions applies in a variety of related situations. First, if the settings don't change much we must change ourselves in the settings. We change who we are by changing what we do. We remind ourselves to keep on changing what we do by modifying ourselves and the settings as much as possible. For example, I suggested that this young man paint the walls of his room and rearrange the furniture in his home. He had a beard that he might consider shaving off or he might change his hairstyle or grow a moustache. Different clothes, trying different foods and altered mealtimes, new hobbies and evening study courses, bathing instead of showering or vice versa, a new exercise program, seeking new friends, a different mattress, different records and musical styles, and so forth could provide reminders that he was different now from when he had gone into the hospital. Always the doing creates the difference. The new doing reminds us of that difference. We are what we do. We cannot shovel away our shadows, but we can build more robust bodies so that our shadows are more robust than before.

My recommendation for the anticipatory anxiety he felt about undertaking a life outside the hospital was to go ahead and be anxious. There was nothing to be done about the worry. Chemical tranquilization would just mask a normal fear about the unknown. He *ought to be* worried about the step he was taking. The worry showed that he recognized the difficulty of the tasks facing him. The anxiety showed that he wanted to do well on the outside, that he wanted to avoid failure. People who leave the hospital nonchalantly may be walking into difficulties without normal anticipation and preparation.

While the natural stress of the upcoming discharge had to be accepted as it was, the upset could be used to keep this young man actively preparing for the big day. He had to arrange for work on the outside. If he wanted to live away from his family then he must find living accommodations. He must develop the skills of cooking, paying bills, shopping, self-care for minor illness, and the like. As he became involved in preparations and training he would find the anticipatory anxiety somewhat reduced, but it should never go away. Only when he had returned to life outside the hospital and succeeded at it would he have the confidence that he could do it. As usual, confidence *follows* success.

Facing the Inevitable

Writing your obituary, epitaph, and eulogy can be a revealing experience. I've done it several times and find it a useful assignment for many of the people with whom I work. The three fundamental principles of the Constructive Living action method of personal management are to accept your feelings, know your purpose, and do what needs doing. The exercise of writing an obituary, epitaph, and eulogy helps us to examine our long-term purposes, our life goals, what needs doing. It is really not so much a way of dealing with our inevitable deaths as it is a way of ordering our lives until then.

Your obituary is the notice that will appear in your local newspaper once you have died. It provides your age and lists your survivors; it may contain your occupation, the cause of death, time and place of services, and your memorable accomplishments. Project your imagination into the future. Where will you be? How are you likely to die? Who will survive you at that time? What will you have accomplished by then? Consider this future event and write a realistic obituary for yourself.

Your epitaph is the pithy sentence or phrase carved on your tombstone. It is the brief summation of your life, the condensation, in words, of your whole being. What memorable statement do you want to leave to the world on your tombstone or memorial tablet? How do you wish to be remembered? To whom will this statement be addressed?

Your eulogy is the longer statement that one or more persons will present publicly at your funeral or memorial service. What will they say about you? Here you can give freer rein to your expectations about the future. Look at the details of where you will live, what sorts of work you will do, with whom you will be living, your temperament, your. favorite foods and reading materials, your financial situation, your philosophical and religious beliefs, your health, and so forth from birth until death.

Now consider for a moment what isn't contained in these documents. What would you have liked to do with your life but didn't? What tasks remained unfinished when you died? What tasks did you fail to begin? What was not in your history that could have been with some effort on your part? What people? What successes? What skills? What travel experiences? Look for the blanks and evaluate what you must do now to begin to fill them before you die.

You may find this exercise depressing; looking at one's prospective death is an unpleasant undertaking for many people. Furthermore, finding that little has been accomplished in one's life may precipitate bitterness and disappointment. But, whatever feelings emerge, you have faced these existential issues--a necessary undertaking. What you do in the years ahead is important. What you are doing right now is even more important. Now is the only time you will ever be given to begin changes that will result in your being at the place where you want to be when you die. What needs to be done? Do it.

We are all going to die. It is important to restimulate awareness of this basic truth over and over. There are a number of characteristic ways of dealing with death; we all use most of them at one time or another. One method is to try to delay it as long as possible--for example, by wearing seat belts, following a health regimen, obtaining proper medical care, and avoiding dangerous situations. Ignoring death--resigning oneself to its inevitability and "forgetting" about it--is another way of dealing with our mortality.

A third strategy is to "grab for all the gusto" of life. "You only go 'round once in this life." Death becomes a marker, a motivator for living one's limited time fully, and an excuse for self-indulgence.   Death also can be reinterpreted intellectually and thus trivialized. There is much talk these days of death being a "natural end point" to life. Philosophically, death is seen as a normal element in nature's evolutionary process, necessary for the survival of the new and for the initiation of variety and change. The awesomeness of one's own death is thus minimized from this verbally-distanced perspective.

Some people compete with death. They tempt it with life-risking activities. Others work hard to win a few points in life before losing the game; they seek to leave their mark on the world before their final play is made. Others distance themselves from death artistically or with social rituals. For example, the Days of the Dead are celebrated in parts of Mexico. Candies are made in the shape of skulls, skeleton puppets dance, paintings with death themes are displayed, songs about death are sung.

Some seek immortality through disciplines or arcane knowledge, faith or social contribution, or some other means. And many hedge their bets by adopting more than one of these methods.

Despite our every effort, we still retain an innate fear of personal death. Gregory Zilboorg wrote that there "always lurks the basic fear of death." Ernest Becker, in *The Denial of Death*, argued that no one is immune from this fear. Morita, too, pointed out this dread of the end point of life. Characteristically, Morita also pointed out its usefulness to the individual and to the species. Unpleasant though it may be to cringe before the notion of termination, this fear prompts not only acts of self-preservation but also self-development and personal achievement. In the early years of the twentieth century Morita had already seen the close relationship between self-protection and actualization. It is not only that we desire to live, but that we desire to live fully, to live well, to live to our maximum capacity. Furthermore, we resist with great energy and determination anything that stands in the way of this living of life to its fullest.

Sometimes such barriers are within ourselves. We struggle with our own emotions and habits of behavior in an attempt to push away the deathlike grip of limited living. That struggle is the main reason for your reading this book. In these writings you find information to help you direct your efforts effectively.

Viktor Frankl, in *Man's Search for Meaning* wrote of tucking our deeds safely into the calendar of the past. I want much the same thing for my students. That is, a year from now they should be able to look back and see how much they did that needed doing in this year--not how much turned out well, or even how much was finally accomplished. It is the quality of the doing in which we take pride. Again, "take pride" isn't the same as "feeling pride" or being boastful about a deed. Taking pride in something is a quality of the act and not a quality of mine as I look back on it. The experience is something akin to watching a professional football player or a symphony conductor. I can respect and admire what they do, even "take pride in it," without claiming credit for their work. The I of the past is someone akin to me, and I care about his historical doing, but he is not me, now.

Why Water Bears No Scars

To some degree we all write the novels of our lives in our minds. We organize our pasts to give ourselves orderly and memorable histories (there are entire psychotherapy systems devoted to that task); we create dramas and villains and elaborate plots. We anticipate new chapters and a variety of endings. And, above all, we create in our minds the character we will play in our life novels.

Life does not come to us in the form of a novel. It doesn't bring the orderliness and consistency of a structured creation. Our minds reorganize experience to fit the scripted form we create for ourselves. That is why we may scar ourselves unnecessarily. We can build in unnecessary pain to our lives by creating tragedies when there are only events, by creating consistently weak and suffering characters when there are only moments and more moments of life experience.

Constructive Living deals with this organizing screen our minds throw up to create life novels. Through Constructive Living we learn to connect more closely with the infinitely more interesting and varied reality that presents itself to us. It is about abandoning the dependence on scripting our lives for suffering and about getting on with living constructively, productively.

The distorted order created by saying, "I am this sort of person," "My past was flawed in such and such a way," "She shouldn't be the way she is," "I'll never become that sort of person," "Life will always bring me these kinds of problems," "There is no future for someone like me," is a fictitious organization of reality created by the mind. Through Constructive Living we consider ways to view reality on a more basic and more flexible level. We offer exercises to actualize those views. This realistic perspective goes a long way toward allowing us to make needed moment-by-moment changes in our lives.

Can you already see that life never presents us with "problems," only with events? Can you already see that the notion of "personality" is a sort of abstracted fiction that doesn't exist in our everyday lives? Can you already see that our memories of the past and our explanations of why we did what we did in the past are oversimplified caricatures of what we were really experiencing then? Can you see that the changeableness that is you need not be bound by labels such as "neurotic" or "lazy" or "coldhearted" or "lonely" or "insecure"? If you already see and live these truths, then there is really no need to read further. You already possess the freedom offered here. You are already freed from your life novel. You are living in reality.

Tokuko Shimbo is the wife of a well-known Morita therapist in Tokyo. She has come to know the principles of Constructive Living intimately. She considers the neurotic people she encounters to be "tone deaf about life (*seikatsu onchi*, in Japanese)." They try to force the natural pitch and rhythm of everyday life into an artificially constructed image of how life ought to be scripted. They force their life-novel scripts on others. They miss the melody of what is.

A rushing stream of water flows around the obstacles that stand in its way. It doesn't stop to dwell on the injuries sustained by a projecting rock or a submerged log. It keeps moving toward its goal, encountering each difficulty as it appears, responding actively, then moving along downstream. The stream has no imagination to create unchanging stories of its existence. It washes away its own wounds in its present purposefulness. Water bears no scars.

V. Neurotic Moments

Ordinary People

The vast majority of people who come for Constructive Living training in life management aren't odd. They don't stand out in a crowd. They do recognize, acutely, that they aren't living up to their potential. They do sense, painfully, life's blows and pressures. On some level they are aware that they cannot make the world into the ideal world they have in mind, so they come to work on themselves. They learn that working on themselves also involves working on the world and changing themselves also results in changing the world. We are linked inseparably with our circumstances. In fact, just starting to study this constructive life process changes our circumstances and so changes us.

Ken lives in his office-warehouse. He rarely leaves it. All around him are reminders of the current sad state of his business. He feels guilty about some of his business practices; he worries about losing money in recent ventures; he despairs when he makes money because of increased income tax assessments; he avoids bringing his accounting system up to date; he feels trapped and isolated and alienated. Ken is miserable. It is a tragic observation that Ken doesn't seem to be miserable enough! If he were suffering more he might get out of his work setting, find an apartment, try some classes at a local community college, join a club, expand his world beyond buying and selling.

The more Ken complains about his circumstances the angrier and more hopeless he becomes. There is initially some release when Ken gets something off his chest, a catharsis. But continued complaining simply makes him a skillful complainer. It is the same, of course, for all of us. One of Ken's assignments, one he frequently forgets, is to refrain from pouring out his troubles to others in his everyday contacts with them. Not only does it become unpleasant for his friends and relatives to listen to his tirades, but it is unproductive for Ken. He must get his mind off himself and onto what must be done to improve his situation. When Ken reverses his habits and becomes a leaning post for others his problems will begin to reduce their dimensions in his mind. Note the order of change that is necessary. It is not that we must somehow straighten out Ken in order to make him worthy of and helpful to others. Instead, Ken must start becoming a listening support to others and then he will begin to straighten out. The constructive doing can actually precede feeling ready to undertake such a self-giving project.

Sol was pressured by a friend to sniff cocaine at a party. Frightened, Sol pretended to try it but concealed the drug and threw it away later. Cocaine would have been an easy temporary escape from misery for this affluent middle-aged bachelor. But something in Sol is willing to endure suffering a bit longer in order to embrace a more constructive solution to his misery. Sol is also resisting pressures from his family to return to live with them and to pursue the career they have selected for him. All this resistance is difficult and painful for Sol. But it reflects a solid core of strength and good judgment that isn't giving in to immediate discomfort.

On the other hand, like Ken, Sol isn't hurting enough. His unpleasant work situation, his lying in bed in the mornings, his failure to seek anything more from women than sexual contacts, his inattention to his physical condition and appearance, and his dependency on his family keep him in a state of suffering that prompts complaints and self-criticism but very little action to change his circumstances. If he were more miserable he might become desperate enough to work himself out of these conditions.

"People are always letting me down," complains Frank. He finds us all lacking. Frank is a fundraiser, middle-aged, with big eyes and a boyish smile. He was a flower child of the sixties grown up into a businessman of the eighties and nineties. He is pulled between the innocent search for some sort of spiritual transcendence and the cutthroat world of moneymaking. Now guilty, now gloating; now seeing through the crap, now diving into it. Frank's LSD insights are sometimes blurred by *el dinero*, but not erased. He longs for something beyond the dollar sign. His life reverberates with disappointment.

When business goes well Frank drifts and drinks and falls behind in his commitments to the world. When his business and personal worlds inevitably collapse Frank hurts and buckles down and catches up on his debts. Then, predictably, life goes pretty well for the next half-cycle.

Sometimes we wonder together, Frank and I, which is better for him--feast or famine? Good times or bad? And we wonder, "Which are the good times?"

Gardening

The old man, bent over by his weeding task, moves slowly from raised row to row. The lettuce and daikon radish and Chinese cabbage are surrounded by the irrepressible optimism of *koa* and nut grass and milkweed. Behind him the beds of yams and peanuts and peas are clear of weeds, the results of yesterday's work. But sprouts of sensitive plant and *koa* and castor bean are already showing among the string beans and Maui onions he had cleared earlier in the week. By the time he works through today's vegetable beds and tomorrow's formations of zinnias, marigolds, and chrysanthemums, the beans and onions will be fighting for existence with their tough, fast-growing weedy competitors.

Always behind, fighting a rearguard action against the invasion, the old man refuses to hurry. Carefully, carefully he pulls each grassy stalk by hand.

"You've gotta get the roots, you know. Break 'em off at the stem and they're up again the next day."

He cannot win this war. The weeds are inexhaustible. Wave after wave they come, borne on the Hawaiian breeze. Still he stoops and plucks them from the earth, protecting his pampered leafy confederates. If you ask him why he doesn't give up his hopeless course and yield to the inevitability of his garden's return to its wild state, he pauses, puzzled for a moment by the question.

"I don't have to work on the whole garden at once," he observes. "just this part, now. Then that part, then the next part, over there. Got these weeds to pull now . . . better get on with it."

He returns to his task. Tonight for dinner he will have onions and beans and yams and fresh peas for his persistence. While he eats, the weeds outside will keep on growing.

I am impressed by the persistence of weeds, but more impressive is the persistence of people who continue to battle the weeds in their lives knowing that there is no end to the task. This true story is about the reassuring prospect that there is only one weed that needs to be pulled at any time.

Where We Live

Marlene complains that she's not earning thirty thousand dollars a year. Irwin worries because he has no paying job at all. Marge is having trouble with her husband. Larry yearns for that promotion. Does it seem strange that I asked all of these people how carefully they brushed their teeth that morning? Who cares about brushing teeth when these major life problems appear? Marlene tells me that if she makes more than thirty thousand dollars in a year, she'll take time to clean her teeth with dental floss, too. But right now, there's no time to waste on such hygienic trivialities.

Despite the commercials for toothpaste to the contrary there is nothing magical about sparkling-white teeth that will attract companions and ensure business success. But those who neglect the details of daily life lose something worth more than thirty thousand dollars. If Marlene does well, with full attention, what life brings to her to do moment by moment, then her salary takes its proper place in perspective. Irwin can find satisfaction in wholeheartedly seeking a job, keeping his appearance neat, even vacuuming the house. Marge will profit from doing her housework well, artfully discussing her dilemma with her husband (whatever he chooses to do about her message), helping the children with their homework, collecting rare coins, finding work outside the home, separating from her spouse, or whatever she decides needs doing.

Often in life we have no direct control over the outcome of major events in our lives. Fate or people in authority over us or the aging process or something else may turn an event one way or another. But life continues to present to us "small" events, chances to control the way we turn on a radio, chances to reach gracefully for the soap in the shower, chances to dust and mend and wash dishes well. Each of these "small" events gives us the opportunity to develop our attention and our character infinitesimally. The accumulated effect is powerful and visible, both to ourselves and to others. Larry may never get the promotion, but he can build himself at the office and at home, whether the promotion comes or not, all the while doing his best to lobby for and deserve the promotion that may come his way.

Why try to base life on what may or may not occur? Why evaluate success in terms of something we cannot completely control? Life is built on moment-by-moment doing. Those moments are all we have. The moment of receiving-that-promotion is only one such moment. To be sure, that moment has implications for what life presents to Larry later on, too. But whatever those implications--if he gets a larger office with a window, for example--there will still be only more moments with different challenges, other opportunities to grow or slip back.

Washing Away Our Scars

Stephen wakes up in the morning feeling like a failure. He wishes the feeling would go away. But Stephen is not living a life that anyone would call successful. The message his mind is sending him seems perfectly appropriate and even positive. That is, his mind is telling him (and me) that it won't be satisfied with the passive, nonconstructive life Stephen is leading. Oddly, I am encouraged by this discomforting communication.

Rather than trying to erase this important message about failure with positive thinking or tranquilizers, I recommend to Stephen that he thank his mind each time that message of dissatisfaction appears. His mind will continue to make him miserable until he changes his actions. After expressing gratitude for the message, he needs to turn immediately to what needs doing right now that will change his failing lifestyle.

At a recent meeting in Japan a young woman asked my advice about her problem with needles and pins. She worries that she has lost a needle somewhere. Even when she counts the needles before and after using them, and she comes up with the same number, she worries that she lost one on an earlier occasion.

I told her that being careful about needles is not her problem. It is a good idea to be careful about them. People who are careless in such matters are likely to find themselves painfully reminded of their negligence. Her problem is in not doing the next thing that needs to be done after checking that she has properly returned all the needles and pins she used during a sewing session.

When she develops the habit of turning to the next task immediately and smoothly, her attention will be drawn into the work or play at hand and won't linger on the past matter of the needles. Although she believes that her difficulty lies in her fixation on the needles, it really lies within the later matter of what she does (or doesn't do). The concern about needles--like the worry before an examination or the anxiety about one's health or the dread of learning to drive or the fear of making a mistake in front of others or the shyness when making a new acquaintance--is natural. Anxiety is natural. Shyness is natural. Anticipatory worry is natural. All feelings are natural. They are only problems when we allow them to hinder what we do. They become problems when we try to struggle with them and try to control them with our will.

A much better strategy--the one I suggested to this young lady--is to accept the concern as it is, as part of her reality at the moment, and get on about the cooking or vacuuming or laundering or dressing for the party or whatever.

Helen tells me her parents don't properly love her. I ask her to look at the specific ways in which her failure to hold down a job, her shyness, and her reluctance to talk to her parents have caused trouble for them. Stacy notes that his wife and children blame him for being either too confining or too lax in the way he disciplines his children. His children show adolescent rebelliousness, and his wife is not the perfect housekeeper he wishes her to be. I ask him to notice the favors these household members bestow on him and to offer a word of gratitude for even the smallest thoughtful deed. Stacy tells me that he already reminds his daughter when she fails to say thank you at an appropriate time. I point out that it is his words of thanks that are at issue here, not his daughter's. He is having no trouble with such matters, he insists. I ask him to go even beyond the level he has achieved so far, to offer verbal appreciation for the slightest effort of his wife and children, no matter whether he truly feels the circumstance to be trivial, no matter whether he sees zero positive response from them for his efforts, no matter whether he is feeling angry or regretful or unappreciated at the time. The form alone is sufficient at this stage of study.

People who suffer a great deal from anxiety may not recognize the inconvenience their problems are causing others around them. Although some of my students are acutely aware of difficulties they cause others (and that awareness adds to their misery), neither those who are aware nor those who are unaware are actively involved in reducing the inconvenience of others.

They are so involved in fighting their own condition that they lack energy and attention to be helpful to others.

Often, I find it useful to recommend that my students reflect on the specific, concrete ways in which their neurotic behavior causes trouble to people around them. At the same time I ask them to pay attention to the efforts of others in their behalf. There is immediate resistance whenever these combined exercises are assigned. Who wants to work on an assignment that will make them feel guilty? What have others ever done for them? Why not work directly on their own personal problem rather than paying so much attention to others? The resistance to these assignments takes many forms: some complain, some forget to carry out the assignments, some forget what the assignments were, some don't return for another session, some simply refuse to consider such a foolish task. But those who diligently look at the troubles they cause others and the favors others are doing for them find the exercise of great value.

Former Students

Fred tells me that the work he put in yesterday on his accounts was "totally wasted." His life is "absolutely awful." He is a "complete failure," "worthless," "suppressed by everything and everybody." Immediately and automatically Fred attaches a strong value label to thoughts as they arise in his mind. This habit of thinking is a combination of a neurotic "all or nothing" attitude and neurotic perfectionism. It is both the cause and effect of an unrealistic view of the world.

A cornerstone of Constructive Living is the attitude of *arugamama*. *Arugamama* is precisely the opposite attitude to that of Fred's. *Arugamama* means accepting reality as it is. The Japanese word itself means literally, "as it is." As reality presents itself to our senses, our minds organize the stimuli into meaningful patterns. Some people have developed the mental habit of attaching extreme value labels and absolutist adjectives to these patterned events. When it is hot, it is "terribly" hot; when it is cold, it is "unbearably" cold. The red light that halts their progress is a "damned" red light. The malfunctioning can opener "never" works right. And so on.

These poor habits of thought interfere with the readiness of the neurotic person to respond promptly and properly to the needs of the situation. Obstacles appear insurmountable, setbacks seem devastating, inconveniences become paralyzing. The first step in changing this unsatisfying orientation is to notice that it occurs. I frequently interrupt Fred's long, complaining monologues to point out his use of absolutes and strong value labels in his speech. Fred is a quick-minded fellow. He begins to notice them and to point them out himself with a small smile of recognition. He begins joining the game of identifying his speech habits.

Habits take time to break, just as they took time to form. So Fred will fall back into neurotic thought patterns again and again before breaking through them. One of the techniques that will help Fred is to present him with new stimuli he hasn't already labeled and dismissed. Fred is self-employed. His business allows him to leave his office and warehouse when he wants, but in fact he stays there, practically lives there, nearly all of his waking hours. I assign long walks, trips to the beach and to local parks, visits to nearby university research libraries. These novel inputs from reality will present Fred with the opportunity to develop the new habits of thinking that we talk about in our sessions.

Much of my work consists of saying the same things over and over again in novel ways so as to hold the attention of my students. Constructive Living theory is not so complex. It is the detailed application of the theory that takes minute attention and persistence. By using a variety of illustrations and analogies I can hold the student's attention and reinforce the points of Constructive Living through repetition. Novelty and surprise are useful tools in getting my job done.

Sal is in his late thirties and not doing much with his life, according to his mother's point of view. She has big plans for Sal. She wants him to go to a university for advanced degrees in engineering. She wants him to wear a white shirt and tie and to work in an office. Sal, on the other hand, enjoys working with his hands. He is a skillful mechanic, in need of the physical activity and concrete problem solving that working on an automobile provide.

Sal isn't stupid. He realizes that he must do what he knows needs to be done, not what his mother has decided for him. He sometimes argues with her over the issue of his career. Sal tries to convince her that she should see things his way. After all, it is his life and his work they are talking about. Sal's mistake is in trying to make his mother satisfied with his choice of occupation. Her opinions are fine just as they are. Sal is trying to accomplish precisely what he objects to in his mother's efforts. He is trying to impose his choice and will upon her. There is no need for them to view this issue with the same eyes. Allowing his mother her own perspective could even provide her with a model for her eventual allowance of Sal's perspective. Confrontation is worse than useless in this situation; it is actually harmful. Acceptance and waiting are more likely to resolve the difficulty. Meanwhile, Sal must go steadily about his chosen work--doing it with attention and craftsmanship without trying to control the uncontrollable.

When Morita was treating a woman with dirt phobia, he took her toothbrush from her after she had used it and, without washing it, brushed his own teeth with it. The patient was shocked to see this highly respected professor of psychiatry using her "contaminated" toothbrush. The impression had such impact that her symptoms were relieved. Once again Morita had demonstrated the importance of action as a teaching device. Verbal instruction and probing insight may be helpful in the resolution of neurotic problems, but they aren't sufficient in themselves, either for the instructor or for the student.

Throughout Constructive Living there are parallels between the instructor's action and attitude and that which is expected from the students in order to surmount their disorders. Constructive Living instructors actually model the lifeway they are recommending to their students.

It is 7:30 A.M. I just finished talking with a student for half an hour on the telephone. Paul called to tell me about how terrible his life is these days. An attorney failed to file some court papers resulting in the loss of thousands of dollars. A worker who was hired to repair some of Paul's property in preparation for selling it doesn't appear to be doing any work, and Paul is having difficulty contacting the man. After working on a number of drafts of a business letter Paul finally called a friend to write it for him. On and on, Paul complains about the poor service he is getting from reality.

I assigned Paul the task of speaking only positively for the rest of the day. We are scheduled for an individual teaching session tomorrow morning. Until that time Paul is to refrain from complaining to anyone about anything. He is to find something positive to say to everyone he encounters. He is to express praise and gratitude to all who come in contact with him today regardless of how he really feels. I instructed him to be an actor, to play a part until the part becomes his reality.

I am instructing Paul to bottle up his dissatisfaction rather than expressing it. I am instructing him to be "unreal" in the sense of acting along lines that aren't in accord with his feelings. My guidance would bring about shocked horror in some therapy circles. But for Paul in this time and in these circumstances such an assignment is appropriate. And Paul himself knows it! He has no trouble expressing his unhappiness about the way the world is treating him. He has been expressive in this way for years--and the complaints have led him into deeper and deeper misery. Paul senses that Constructive Living's approach offers a way out of his negativism. In the past when Paul was true to his feelings, he was only acting in concert with *some* of his feelings, the ones he chose to focus on, the negative ones. There are other feelings in Paul that have been ignored and underplayed. Those feelings accompany desires to grow and give to others and stretch out his life in a more positive direction. We shall see how much effort he puts into practicing the assignments. Again, it is the doing that will change Paul's feelings and not vice versa.

VI. NEUROTIC MISTAKES

Public Misconceptions

A recent magazine ad reads:
"Barbara's problem isn't her weight. Her weight is only a symptom. A symptom of a serious illness. She's physically addicted to food and psychologically obsessed with it.
"She doesn't need more diets. She needs professional medical care."

It is hard to accept the idea that anyone could believe such foolishness. Barbara's problem is her weight. Better yet, the photograph shows that Barbara is fat. Barbara is better off facing the reality that confronts her than hiding behind some ludicrous pseudomedical label of illness. She may have other problems, too, of course. But to attempt to define them all as medical problems is to make all of life medical. She does need a diet, and exercise. She needs to change what she eats and how much she eats and, probably, when she eats. Her problem of overweight is no more medical than the problem of laziness or pessimism or criminality.

We are all "physically addicted to food." We had better be if we wish to stay alive. We all become psychologically obsessed with food when we haven't eaten for a long while.

Barbara's problem is neither addiction nor obsession. She eats too much; she exercises too little or improperly. Let's be realistic.

Alcoholism, too, has come to be mislabeled as illness by some, as has neurosis. I wait for the ad programs that will promote a treatment for the "illness of jealousy," or "Cure bad penmanship medically!" or "Enter Lawngreen Hospital and overcome your laziness." It is all too easy to sidestep responsibility for what we do by labeling our problem an illness, a medical problem. But it is sheer absurdity.

Seeking the Magical Brazier

How desperately and persistently my students seek salvation outside of themselves! They are certain that there is some wonderful warming current that will melt the ice in their lives for them. Sometimes they try to put me in the role of savior. Such effort always leads to disappointment. I never saved anyone. Until the students learn to melt into reality they remain frozen hard in their self-consciousness:

If I changed my therapist perhaps I'd get better.

If I moved closer to (farther from) my work (my lover, that nicer section of town, a religious facility, the hospital) life would go well for me.

If I took the right combination of medications (vitamins, herbs) all the trouble with my emotions would go away.

If my family (the bank, my boss) gave me the money I need to start over I wouldn't have any more problems.

If I changed jobs (lovers, dreams) all would be fine.

If I could just find a good man (woman) I could settle down and my worries would be over.

If I felt better (had more confidence, worried less, felt braver, loved myself more) I'd make some solid changes in my life.

The search for sources of salvation never ceases. When I challenge the search itself my student may become quite emotional, There is some comfort in believing that there exists somewhere a saving condition, whether it is in our grasp or not. Unfortunately (or fortunately), there is no salvation from outside. There is only acceptance and proper action. There is only holding to purpose through storms of emotion. There is only understanding and acting based on best knowledge. The soft padding is gone, but the resources are sufficient and dependable, in time.

Putting Life Off until Tomorrow

One of our Constructive Living maxims is "Don't put your life on hold." While waiting for the results of a job interview or an examination, or even while stopped at a stoplight or waiting for the water in the teapot to boil or waiting for a computer to boot up or an Internet document to download, some people seem to turn off their minds, to drift along without noticing what reality is sending them during those "in-between" moments. Every moment is worthy of full attention and dedicated action;

every moment holds the potential for use in building a character that is "realistic" in the finest sense of that word.

Putting off unpleasant or difficult tasks is a similar sort of habit with dysfunctional consequences. Not long ago a leaky radiator shot steam into a room in my home while I was out of town. I returned to find the paint peeling and flaking off the walls. The support for a drapery rod had pulled loose from its anchor in the plaster. This situation is typical of the sort of task that won't go away; the room won't repair itself however much I might wish it to do so. Procrastination would simply add to my discomfort because I would be repeatedly reminded of the difficult work awaiting me; the unsightly wall would reappear each morning, and the struggle to get myself to do the task would take up increasing amounts of energy. In this case, there were a couple of days in which I had other commitments, so I was unable to get to the repair work immediately. On and off during those intervening days I felt rather out of sorts, recalling the scraping, repainting, and repairs that lay ahead.

The project took almost an entire day, but the result was rewarding, and the mental burden of the unaccomplished task, which had been carried for two days, disappeared. Reality doesn't bring us things to do according to some ideal schedule that we have planned in our minds. Sometimes it seems to be at the most inconvenient time that we are presented with a task that requires immediate attention. Cars break down, roofs leak, friends cry, weeds grow, dust accumulates, correspondence piles up, bills arrive, guests appear, and so forth. Jumping into reality, acting as the moment requires, eliminates some of the unnecessary suffering that accompanies procrastination and wishing that life were otherwise. Involvement in the doing not only moves us toward achievement of the immediate project, but it also distracts our attention from the foolish and unnecessary habit of focusing on our miserably bad luck.

We alone create neurotic struggles in life. Reality merely presents issues and problems for resolution. The neurotic struggles we experience are internal evaluations that we add to the circumstance presented to us. No architect ordains I will face 117 pleasant life operations and 114 unpleasant ones today. They simply come as they come and I define them so. Although we require challenges to live at our peak, to define these experiences as struggles and regret their persistence is unnecessary; it is our response to them that is vital.

To wait when action is necessary is a failure to respond to the needs of the situation. But, to act when waiting is the better solution is no better. Like many Westerners, I tend to lean toward action when inaction is more appropriate. I want a response from the world in my time frame, at my convenience. To be sure, I am willing to work hard to get the results I hope for. But working hard at waiting is difficult.

Notice I am careful to write about waiting and inaction rather than writing about patience. It is true that I'm too often impatient. But patience is a feeling or an attitude or a state of mind. Patience is something that we have or don't have in any given moment. I can't create patience by my will any more than I can create love or courage. And you can't either. Patience may be developed indirectly through the act of waiting again and again. Patience is acquired over time, through attention to what we do. As we prune and nurture certain deeds, we indirectly influence what we think and feel. Thus, we change who we are. Patience is no different from other feelings. It is developed by selectively doing. By waiting, we make ourselves into more patient people.

The kind of patience that we aim for in Constructive Living may be called "productive" patience. It is based upon productive waiting, which means being active in another area while waiting for some desired result. It means keeping our eyes off the pot that hasn't yet boiled. It means allowing our friends and mates time to work through their own thoughts and feelings and not forcing them to deal with issues according to our own timetables, our own convenience. It means allowing the glue we call "time" to set completely before testing it.

Productive waiting means asserting ourselves when necessary, but then coolly evaluating the outcome of our efforts and deciding what needs to be done next. Just as important, productive waiting means going about other business and play, while the situation is ripening. It means turning away fully, involving ourselves wholeheartedly in some other pursuit, until the proper time comes to resume the attack on the problem. It means overcoming our obsessions with our own personal time constraints, our own concerns, and our own convenience.

By "our own convenience" here I am contrasting more than simply our own personal convenience with that of some other person. The world about us has a timetable of its own. Events ripen at their own pace. Traffic moves along the freeway independent of my appointments and desires. I can choose to turn onto side streets if freeway traffic gets bottled up. But if I choose to stay on the freeway, I cannot ignore the speed of the cars around me moment by moment.

Perhaps some of you are expecting to read here some tips about how to comfortably and skillfully go about practicing this productive waiting. If so, I must disappoint you. I know of no easy way to keep my mind off those chocolate chip cookies baking in the oven. I have found, though, that putting my body in another room in front of some absorbing task makes the waiting somewhat more bearable. I have found also that the more I see productive waiting in actual living situations, the more I notice the payoffs, and the more I am willing to give this kind of waiting a try. Still, there is nothing I know of that makes waiting comfortable or easy in all situations.

I'll express it again: Constructive Living suggestions for living don't make life easy, but they make it sensible, and they put a handle on what is controllable in life. I mistrust anyone who offers constant happiness, endless success, instant confidence, or effortless self-growth. Somehow, those offers never get delivered.

Heads You Lose, Tails You Lose

I just had a call from a client who was feeling terrible because the cashier at the Motor Vehicle Department treated him so well. He was certain that he didn't deserve such kind treatment.

"I wonder how you would have felt if she had treated you badly," I mused.

"Probably terrible," he confessed.

I suspect he was right. He has set up a no-win situation for himself.

The late Dr. Takehisa Kora, a prominent Morita therapist in Tokyo, told the story of a patient who came to him complaining that he feared going insane. Kora examined the man and explained that he wasn't going insane, rather he was suffering from a sort of phobia about going insane. He also told the patient that people who actually do go insane generally do so without awareness, and those who worry about insanity never go crazy; worrying in that characteristic way is almost a guarantee that it won't happen. The man felt reassured.

However, a couple of weeks later the patient returned with a new complaint.

"I'm not so anxious now about going crazy. So I wonder if I'm not in danger now of really going crazy."

Heads he loses, tails he loses.   Newness and change provoke no-win responses from some people. They are uncomfortable in their current situations, but they dread the unknown elements of change, too. To stand still is to be in pain; to move is to create pain.

One professor I know had an irrational fear that by reading high-level theoretical material he would be caught up in a world of intriguing ideas and so lose touch with reality. He recognized that the fear was probably groundless, but it was the very "groundlessness" that left him trembling with fascination and terror. If he didn't keep up to date, he was doomed professionally. If he read, he risked drifting off into ethereal realms, permanently.

What these people have in common is that they let their thinking freeze their action. They are immobilized by trying to take into consideration what might happen. They want to figure out all the angles beforehand. They want to be assured that every future step is safe, pain free. But life offers no such guarantees. So what can they do?

They must act anyway, without confidence, without assurance, without a clear view of all possible outcomes. We don't need to know everything about everything before putting our bodies in motion. Careful consideration is worth our time and attention, but straddling the fence waiting for everything to become absolutely clear and perfectly safe offers only saddle sores. If you are in pain, take the constructive step into the unknown and discover what reality has in store for you in the next moment.

On General Principles

Professor Anees Sheikh tells the story of a young student from India who came to visit the United States. He was accustomed to brewing tea from loose tea leaves, so when a tea bag was given to him he began to tear it open. His host told him that in America we simply drop the whole tea bag into our cup. So, having learned his lesson, he picked up a packet of sugar and...you know the rest of that story.

What the student did makes some sense. He continued to operate on the principle of "not tearing." But the results weren't as expected. His behavior turned out to be unrealistic. We need to keep checking out what we do against the standards of reality. But some people try to figure out much of reality in their minds, without acting on it. Because they fail to observe what really is, they expect reality to be like their fantasies and imaginings.

As noted above, Yozo Hasegawa pointed out that we can be obsessed with positive objectives as well as neurotic concerns. He talked about the obsession of some salaried men with their work and the similarity of that obsession to being "caught" by neurotic symptoms. Both neurotic people and workaholics show a kind of inflexibility, a poor adaptation to the reality that presents itself to them. People can be obsessed with all sorts of things--by succeeding, by making money, by being in love, by their faults, by studying, by sex, by neurotic tendencies, by their work, by self development, and so forth. None of these interests is bad in itself. There is nothing wrong, for example, with wanting to be successful or free of faults. The problem is the being caught, the *toraware*, which freezes attention on the obsession and turns us away from the open acceptance of reality.

I would suggest that we go even further theoretically. It is not the neurosis that we correct by Constructive Living, but the *toraware* itself. Neurotic symptoms are no better or worse than the desire to succeed, the impulse to study, or the dream of buying a new home. It is the obsession with any of these that needs to be corrected. The obsession narrows the thinking and separates the person from reality. When we focus exclusively on an obsession (such as trying to get rid of neurotic symptoms or trying to succeed in our profession) we cannot see the reality around us. We cannot see what properly needs to be done in each moment. It is the obsession itself, that is the difficulty.

People can be stuck on images or stereotypes, too. For example, some Japanese seem to think that Americans must be tall, sexy, assertive, open-hearted, drinkers of alcohol and coffee, eaters of great quantities of bread. They think all Americans have swimming pools in their back yards and home barbecues every weekend. A Japanese friend (whose house I had visited numerous times) made me an especially long *futon* quilted bedding because I am a foreigner and so must be tall. Salespeople suggest large sizes in shirts and suits and slacks because I am a foreigner. In fact, I am about the same height as the average Japanese male, wear medium-size Japanese clothing, rarely eat bread, and don't drink alcohol or coffee. Many foreigners simply don't fit the stereotype Japanese have of them. Just as many Japanese don't fit the stereotype Americans have of them. Most Japanese don't eat sushi every day, rarely wear geta (wooden clogs), and don't carry a camera around with them. Some Japanese sleep in a bed, not on a floor mat and *futon*; their homes have carpets as well as tatami-mat rooms, and so forth.

There are stereotypes of women, too, that produce a kind of *toraware*. Many Japanese people think that women should be housewives, staying at home to raise children, shy, uninterested in politics or economics, experts in shopping and flower arrangement and tea ceremony. Actually, many women in Japan are now working outside the home (at least part time), some are choosing not to marry, some are successful in business and politics and sports. Some women are choosing to move beyond the narrow limits of stereotypes. So the stereotypes will change little by little in Japan just as they have been changing in the United States.

General principles can be useful tools for direction in everyday life. But we must periodically check them against reality. We cannot afford to let ourselves become rigidly attached to principles, attitudes, and ideas that no longer fit reality (if they ever did). Constructive Living aims not so much at perfect consistency or unchanging perfection, but at flexible, natural realism.

Blind Spots

Some people are hurting so badly that they want to be like everyone else. They are mistaken in two ways. They think that others don't hurt, at least in the same ways and to the same extent that they do. And they think that they can become like everybody else.

They have no choice but to be different (we're all different, unique), but they have a choice in determining the direction of that difference. They have the abilities to go beyond the average, to actually live superior lives.

Nowadays, Connie can laugh at the excuses she makes for her successes. She was never one to excuse her failures. Failures seemed natural and inevitable to Connie. They were properly understood by her weakness, her faults, and her neurotic personality--or so she thought. But successes required special explanations, even excuses.

When she was able to sign her name for credit card purchases without trembling it had to be because the salesperson wasn't looking her way and her friend was off browsing in another part of the store. When she was praised for her fine work she believed that her manager had simply overlooked the mistakes that she must have made. When life went smoothly for awhile it was because of unusual circumstances, the efforts of others, a temporary lull in her nervousness, mistakes that slipped by unnoticed, the temporary influence of Constructive Living in her life, and so on and on. Success wasn't natural; failure was.

The tendency is still there after five sessions of Constructive Living coaching. But she notices it, catches herself doing it, and laughs. She has reached an important stage. It is a stage similar to that reached by Charlie.

Charlie criticizes himself unmercifully. In his daily journal he berates himself for the pep talks he uses to psyche himself into getting up, going for a run, getting to work on time, and almost every activity in which he engages. He catches himself not noticing his surroundings. He uncovers his tendency to daydream. He spots his jealousy and dissatisfaction with what he has achieved in comparison with what his peers are achieving.   I

What Charlie is only beginning to see is that his noticing these quirks is an important step in changing them. Before his encounter with Constructive Living, he simply imagined his way through life, stumbling, marking time, lying where he fell. All the time he felt a sometimes vague and sometimes sharp uneasiness. Life ought to be better than the way he was living it. His self-criticism was blurred and pervasive. Now it is sharp and focused. Now it is clearer what needs to be done to change the way he lives.

I keep telling Charlie that this catching himself in sloppy living is a very positive step for him. Miyamoto Musashi, the famed Japanese swordsman, really meant it when he wrote that "The Way is in training." Training doesn't lead to or result in finding the Way to swordsmanship or life. Training, in itself, is already being on the Way. That subtle alteration in attention which allows us to catch our minds trying to con us or run along in old unconstructive habitual ruts is being on the Way. The same process of bringing attention back again and again to the focal breathing or mantra or counting or whatever during meditation can be applied to daily living. We examine what we attend to and get on about doing what needs doing. Such is the Way.

Charlie used to see only the painfulness of the self-criticism. Connie used to see the naturalness of her failure alone. Blind spots. Charlie wanted to eliminate the self-criticism. Connie wanted to eliminate the failure. Why not recognize the usefulness of both and learn from them? Connie can learn the naturalness of success and of change in general by expanding her attitude toward the naturalness of failure. Charlie can learn that his discoveries of momentary slips mean not only failure but successful monitoring, correcting, and steps along the Way.

Failure and self-criticism aren't pleasant. They are downright painful. But they aren't "bad." They aren't best handled by wiping them out, even if we could. They teach us. They are to be used for our growth. Yes, they even deserve our thanks. Blind spots only occur in relationship to certain points of view. Looked at from another perspective a blind spot disappears. Whether it is a stop sign hidden by a willow branch or a truth hidden by pain, there is a place from which reality can be clearly seen.

The Appeal of Pessimism

I can see two attractions of pessimism. Firstly, when things go wrong, at least the pessimists can claim they expected the worst and they were right. Secondly, on television and in movies just when life goes well for the hero, just when misfortune is unexpected, something terrible happens. There may be some expectation among pessimists that always anticipating the worst can magically prevent unfortunate events from occurring. Both of these measures aim at cutting anticipated losses, losses that might not even occur. But such a purpose is the basis of any insurance. The problem with pessimism is that the premiums are very high.

Of course, strictly speaking, there are no pessimists, only people who have frequent moments of pessimism. No one can be negative all the time. And everyone has moments of expecting the worst. Habits of attitude aren't easily changed. Constructive Living suggests we use the information our minds send us, however negative or unpleasant, to assist us in behaving positively and constructively. If you worry that your roof might be leaking, check it. If you feel gloomy about your job prospects, work to improve them.

We do, however, sometimes feel pessimistic about conditions we can't do anything about. If you know something about Constructive Living then you can guess the approach we recommend in such situations. When you can't do anything to change the circumstances, then you accept the circumstances as they are, you accept the pessimistic feelings associated with them, you accept your dislike of feeling pessimistic, you accept your dissatisfaction with all this accepting, you accept your tendency to analyze this whole situation. And, meanwhile, you get on with doing what can be done in your life. Optimistic or pessimistic, clever or foolish, thoughtful or thoughtless, eager or reluctant, active or passive--we are all of these at one moment or another. Constructive Living won't make you optimistic; it doesn't need to do so. Just doing well what reality sends to be done is sufficient. Issues of optimism and pessimism and the like will wither away from inattention.

I Alone Suffer

There is a common myth that no one suffers like we do and no one can understand our suffering. Each of my beginning students is likely to believe that he or she suffers uniquely and alone and more than other people.

Rev. Shue Usami, head of Senkobo Temple in Mie Prefecture in Japan, tells about a man who complained to his doctor, "I suffer so much from this operation." His doctor's reply was, "Yes, we all suffer from your operation--your family, your nurses, and I do, too." The patient considered only his own distress. The doctor reminded him that others shared his distress, too. His family was worried and inconvenienced by their visits to the hospital; the doctor had to stay up the night after the operation to watch his patient's progress; the nurses were called upon for extra vigilance and special care. It is rare to suffer alone. The wavelets of our misery extend to other pools.

Whether my students are challenging cancer or fears of leaving the house, whether they struggle with torturing memories or abusive spouses, they benefit from being able to see the interlocking circles of shared suffering of which they are a part. As always, the primary benefit is straightforwardly seeing more of reality, the way things are. That realistic view is in itself vital for our mental health. In addition, the recognition that we don't hurt alone can bring some measure of relief from feelings of isolation and alienation. Furthermore, concern with others' suffering and our attempts to alleviate it offer an opportunity for selfless action which distracts us from self-focused misery.

Some people seem to build their social identity on their degree of suffering. Their "claim to fame" rests on tragedy after tragedy. They are like children who compare the scabs and scrapes on their knees to see who has the worst. We all have scrapes on our knees. Scrapes, too, are nothing special.

How can we prepare ourselves and our students for the occasional inevitable failure? Life brings us all sorts of challenges; sometimes we rise to the occasion, sometimes not. When a student fails to complete an assignment there may be self recrimination and reverberations of past failures and inadequacy. The Constructive Living position on missed assignments is the same as that of any other situation--what needs to be done now? Reality just keeps coming.

We can respond to a mistake with the emotion-laden reaction "Oh, no! Failed again!" or we can respond with attention to the nature of the new situation presented by our mistake and what needs to be done about it. In general, we work to replace the domination of a feeling response with a reasonable action response. The feeling response doesn't disappear altogether, but it no longer is the primary focus of our attention.

Failure, suffering, dilemmas, crises--all are part of human existence. They are not the whole of it. Our understanding of them and our response to them lie within our control. What needs doing next?

I used to think that some people were born with common sense and some were born without it. Now I know that common sense is earned by many experiences and many failures.

Facts of Life

Disorder myths

A recent advertisement in a popular magazine asks if the reader eats too much, then diets, fasts, or vomits. The ad continues: "You may have thought it was your fault. But it isn't. Chances are you have an eating disorder. And if you do, no amount of willpower will help you control it."

The ad is wrong. The only thing that will control overeating is to eat less. In our strange folk way of talking we say that we eat less because of willpower. Willpower is no explanation; it is just another way of saying we eat less. To label something "an eating disorder" makes it no more medical than to label jealousy "an emotional disorder" or to label filth "a bathing disorder" or to label smoking or drinking alcohol "an addictive disorder" or to label poor manners "an etiquette disorder." They are all the same in that they share problems of behavior, of doing. They are brought under control by doing something differently. You know that.

But we hope to suffer from something easily corrected, something "curable" through medical or psychological magic. A pill, perhaps, or a few sessions with a professional whose expertise will make our problem disappear like a bad dream would be just right. It is time to grow up and face the real situation. When we have behaved ourselves into destructive habits we must behave ourselves out of them. There is no psychological sorcery which will make it easy for us to change what we do. But change we must if we are to be the best we can be.

Costly and time-consuming analysis of the *sources* of our "disorders" is rather interesting. It provides reasons (read "excuses") for our problems; most of these reasons lie outside of our control. How reassuring to believe that the origins of our limitations are someone else's errors (poor parenting, perhaps, or a sick society)! Still, it remains for us to change what we do.

Well, then, how do we begin to change our poor habits of behavior? How do we develop this magical willpower to bring about changes in what we do? Frankly, I have no idea. The process is so complicated. I suspect no one else knows either, though some claim to have mastered the understanding of this elusive matter. What I do know is what needs doing. What needs doing is to have a goal, to accept whatever uncontrollable factors that come along to help or hinder in achieving that goal, and to work toward that goal the best we can. In other words, 1) know your purpose, 2) accept reality (including your circumstances, your parents, your history, and your feelings, along with the rest of reality), and 3) do what needs doing. If you have been studying the Constructive Lifeway you have heard this advice over and over again.

The way it is

No matter what personal growth method or psychotherapy you may try many of life's tasks will never become fun. Taking in the car for servicing, sending off an application for a school transcript, studying an uninteresting subject in school, waiting for the plumber to arrive, cleaning up a spilled bowl of soup-- these activities aren't pleasurable whether or not one is enlightened. To expect some discipline or philosophy to make them enjoyable is rather childish. But do them we must. Enjoyable or not.

Conversely, to try to assert that sexual gratification or eating one's favorite foods or experiencing the rush of an illicit drug isn't pleasurable is equal foolishness. We cannot dictate our feelings one way or the other. We must accept them as they are and still get the car serviced, refrain from overeating, study the uninteresting material, and avoid the chemicals that harm us. No elaborate definitions or theories will make hard struggle easy.

Reality and talk about reality

My impression is that most people want change in their lives because they haven't mastered who they are now or where they are now, because they're not doing well with what they have. How about mastering what is now and then changing?

I sometimes see "healers" trying to force their clients' words and lives into some prearranged schema. The schema are more or less complicated, but they are limited conceptual models of what reality ought to be. Reality isn't any of their models. To the extent that a healer realizes this truth, the healer is wise.

Ideas about living well are useful and worth our attention, but so is the rest of reality.

Constructive Living suggests that it is better to master the simple levels of encountered reality before trying to understand or master more complex ideational schemes. I suspect that high-level philosophical word play gets society's attention and rewards because it helps distract people from ineptness at doing well in concrete, everyday reality. It is easier to ponder the meaning of life than to fold towels neatly over and over again.

Whether we are drunk or sober, failing or succeeding, reality keeps steadily on. Whatever philosophers or gurus or seers say, reality keeps steadily on. Solid, reliable reality. The word, "reliable," here has a particular meaning. Don't misinterpret it.

Fundamentals

Some people try to make Constructive Living a strategy for temporarily accepting the naturalness of feelings while working to "improve" themselves so that feelings of anger, frustration, lack of confidence, despair and the like don't occur (or are reduced) in their lives. They both lie to themselves and miss the point. Feelings are natural. This moment's feelings fit this moment's me-reality; they are a natural element in this now.

Some Constructive Living students define their life crises as exceptional cases falling outside the realm of a constructive life. They want to call "time out" and return to old ways of handling their current dilemma. They lose the sound basis for action provided by Constructive Living. They don't see that a life crisis fits their practice just like keeping a Constructive Living journal or working on a Constructive Living puzzle-koan or dusting or driving. There is something to be done about the reality which includes the crisis that faces them. Accept reality; know purpose; take action.

Too often we seem to substitute theory for action. And our theories become further and further separated from everyday reality. In psychology, for example, we have elaborate theories about subtle functions of the mind, but some fundamental principles are not taught. For example, some basic principles that aren't taught include the truths that feelings fade over time, feelings keep changing (the feeling that you feel now is not the same feeling you felt in the past, though it may be similar and it may remind you of, say, a childhood feeling), nearly all behavior is directly controllable and feelings are not.

In religion we have both intricate theological theories and personal-experiential approaches to God but little apparent awareness of Reality's contributions to our everyday existence. There is little emphasis on the concrete support we get from other people every day, little attention to the fact that our very existence depended and depends on others' efforts in our behalf. In sociology we have complex theories of social interaction, but our society suffers from social problems which could be solved with the knowledge we have already. In economics we have abundant theories on macro and micro levels but we have a huge national debt and an unbelievable amount of personal debt.

Why is it that we have skipped fundamental truths about action and Reality in order to develop complicated theories based on constructions of the mind and society?

On Alcohol and Other Drugs

My basic objection to alcohol and other drugs is that they interfere with our perception of reality. Constructive Living is about living the best one can within reality. Reality may not be what we wish or what we believe ought to be. But stuffing our minds in some idealized or fantasized space for long periods doesn't help us cope with or change reality. In fact, teasing oneself with alcohol and other drugs may result in very real consequences such as auto accidents, poor job performance, and broken homes. You know that.

The other danger of these chemical pursuits of unreality is that they encourage feeling-centeredness. They may make one feel good, temporarily. So they encourage the user to try to build life on feelings. We know that feelings are uncontrollable directly by the will. Therefore, a feeling-centered life is always in jeopardy; it can't be successfully lived with consistency.

Sometimes we feel good, even ecstatic, sometimes not. Up and down, up and down.

Behavior is controllable, no matter what you hear from alcoholics and addicts. They can stop their self-destructive behavior. And the stopping itself demonstrates to them and to us the freedom we all share. With that freedom comes the chance to live a life based on something controllable, stable. There won't be the momentary chemical highs of the past, and there won't be the desperate, urgent, helpless suffering in between. There is no once-and-for-all-time decision involved here. There aren't even a lot of daily decisions. There is just doing something else other than abusing chemicals. The result is simply the satisfaction of living this moment well, and this moment, and this moment.

Realism

Anyone who has spent years working in a garden or in the fields knows impermanence intimately. We see the cycle of seasons, the coming and going of insects, droughts, freezes, rot, the seeds that sprout or die, the life cycles of plants, the bountiful harvests and the lean ones. It is all change. There is nothing that can be counted on with certainty to be exactly as it was last year. Our only recourse is to keep on fitting what we do, adapting who we are, to the constantly changing circumstances. It does no good to tell the grasshopper eating the soybean leaves, "You really shouldn't be doing that." Wishing the rain would stop (or come) doesn't affect the weather or the plants. Analyzing how we feel about fungus doesn't save the cabbage. We need a more realistic perspective and straightforward action to have a chance to effect the changes we desire.

I am not being passive or resigned when I emphasize the changeableness of the world and the necessity of our adapting to it. Only when we have a clear vision of this flux and our place in it does our effort mean something. To work and succeed and play and love while pretending it will all last, while ignoring the fragile "momentariness" of it all, is to miss the chance for depth in all these activities. To try while dying, to love while changing, to play while acknowledging the impermanence allows a kind of nobility to the simplest act. We surmount that which was only childish escape before.

There is nothing ennobling about suffering itself. But in striving while suffering we move beyond ourselves to become new creatures, whether the striving attains what we set out to accomplish or not. Pain and self-doubt and fear and anger don't necessarily stimulate growth, but they do permit it--when the effort is there. Change is inevitable. In the garden, in us. Some of the change we can influence, some we cannot. Our fundamental hope lies in affecting the change that is us.

VII. CONSTRUCTIVE LIVING REFLECTION

Misalignments

Ten years or so ago I wrote a small book with a vignette about a little girl in Kamakura who was crying to be allowed back into her house. She had done something wrong, and she was put outside the house as punishment. She stood pounding on the front door, tearfully begging to be allowed into the house. I contrasted this Japanese girl's plight with that of the American child who is forced to stay in his or her room as punishment. The American child is not allowed out of the house. The Japanese girl saw her mother and her home as the source of life's rewards; she wanted to be inside the house. The American child sees the unrestrained freedom of play outside as desirable. The reality is somewhat more complicated than this simple contrast, but the story called attention to some differing tendencies between the two countries that seem to be valid.

Later, I saw the same vignette in the writings of a Japan specialist. I was not quoted or credited. For a moment I was miffed, then I recalled that the credit for the story wasn't mine. Should I have credited the little girl? Her family? Those who taught me the Japanese language so that I could understand what she was saying between sobs? The editor and publisher of the book in which the vignette appeared? The government agency that funded that first period of research in Japan? Without any one of these people (and a host of others) there would have been no story to tell. How narrowly self-centered to think that the story could be "mine." What about your marriage, your project, your child, your development, your success?

I made a similar mistake the other day as I turned off the cold water faucet. At first I started to turn to a brief task while allowing the water to run in the sink. Then I stopped and turned off the water, thinking all the while what a conscientious person I am. It is wrong to refrain from wasting water because I want to consider myself a good person. It is proper to turn off the water because the water "deserves" to be used carefully, with attention (and, when it happens naturally, with gratitude). We do what is right because it is right--not because we are fine people, not because God will punish or reward us, not because of sheer habit, not to show off our proper upbringing, not to atone for our sins--just because it is right.

I began reading David Viscott's book about how to conduct the business aspects of psychotherapy. In Taking Care of Business, Viscott honestly and straightforwardly points out that psychotherapy is a business, and he goes on to offer advice on how to run that business properly and successfully. His candor is admirable. In Viscott's book the most useful revelation for me was that I am not in the business of psychotherapy. I am in the business of trying to repay the world for my existence. It is nice to receive fees and royalties and honoraria. But Constructive Living is more important than a means of making a livelihood. It is the means of making a life, a whole life. And the financial aspect of that whole life waxes and wanes in importance from moment to moment. The debts I owe aren't merely financial. Constructive Living is more than making a living; it's my life.

Warming Trend

Today I crossed the street without waiting because a man had already pushed the traffic button for pedestrians. He had been waiting for the cycle to turn the light red and stop the cars. I walked up just as the cars came to a halt. I was grateful that his waiting had expedited my crossing.

Perhaps some Westerners would wonder at my sense of gratitude. He pushed the button so that he could cross the street and not for my convenience. Of course. Yet I did, in fact, benefit from his action. To be sure, my benefit did not appear to be his intent. Still, his action served me, whatever his intent. Where should we draw the line of thanks? People buy my books not to support me, but the result is that I am supported. Do they deserve my thanks? Yes, I believe that they do. Salespeople sell shoes to customers in order to make their living. Do they merit my appreciation even though I paid for the shoes? Yes, they do.

Democratic capitalism has become a sort of self-centered enterprise. The theory is that some balance can be achieved if all of us act in our own self-interest. The theory is that when I exceed my bounds your self-interest will push me back into line. Theory holds that no one can expect that you will sacrifice your success for my convenience. A chilling wind drifts through the crevices of this socioeconomic system. It ignores the perspective that I owe you something even though I have paid a fair price for your service. You owe me something for asking you to serve me. We are favoring each other with our business on a dimension other than the one of economic transaction.

We all sense this difference between balanced self-interest and the dimensions of human favor. That is why we prefer to shop at stores where the employees and management seem actually grateful for our patronage. It is why we feel offended by postal employees who act as though they do us a favor by selling postage stamps. Mutual gratitude glides along above an exchange of equal economic value, making the transactions shine and making us more than mere mechanisms of economic exchange.

Again, whether or not those who do me favors (knowingly or not, intentionally or not) reciprocate my gratitude, my words of thanks are due them.

I'm grateful to my toothpaste for cleaning my teeth and to the manufacturer for making the toothpaste. In our society the consumer is often seen to be aligned against the producer (as labor is aligned against management). It is refreshing to consider the service I receive and the debt I owe to those whose products ease and enrich my life.

This attitude is part of the treasuring of all things because all things are borrowed. There is nothing that is truly mine. What I bought was paid for with money received from others. The money was earned with my time and effort; but these outputs, too, are possible only because of the training I received from others, the food prepared by others, the body that was a gift from my parents, and so forth. As I trace back everything that appears to be "mine" it evaporates into the plethora of debts I owe the world.

Taking it a step further I am but a reflection of these efforts of others. I am the product of my surroundings, surroundings that extend back in time to eras before my birth. How much I owe to Edison and Lincoln and Columbus and Plato and some unnamed protohominid ancestor, to those who sowed and sewed and so kept my ancestors alive, to the corn and cotton, the sun, the melting snow. Back and back, the closer I look the wider the net of interconnections--it is less a widening tunnel of gratitude than an embracing totality that exists now and extends into past and future, equally encompassing.

It seems appropriate to say that I am my surroundings. What is there that is mine that is separate from them? For this moment I become you, too. Thank you for your contribution to this part of this moment/circumstance that I call "me."

On Realistic Gratitude

Gratitude is a feeling and so is uncontrollable directly by our will. We cannot generate gratitude simply by telling ourselves to be grateful. On the other hand, however, gratitude is a natural response to keeping our eyes open as we operate in the world. It takes a certain amount of effortful blindness to miss the truth of Reality's moment-by-moment support of our lives. From the oxygen we breathe to the efforts of others who provide our food and our stereos, our comfort and our education, our livelihood and our sports partners, we "are lived" by Reality.

Constructive Living holds that the realistic gratitude we experience as we take notice of the supportive nature of our world carries with it a desire to repay the world somehow and a certain degree of sadness or guilt that we aren't doing more along the lines of balancing our debts to the world.

I am not interested in arguing these points. I take them as self evident. At this moment in time you either understand and recognize what I have written here or you don't. If you give this lifeway a serious try, you will come to insights of the sort mentioned above. Beware that you don't walk in a direction leading toward an undesired goal.

One learns about Reality (and oneself as part of Reality) by acting in it. Everyday life is our best teacher. By directing and noticing what we do in our daily lives we learn about ourselves. By paying attention to what Reality sends our way we learn about Reality.

Some of my students talk a great deal about knowing themselves. They have invested long periods of time in analyzing their thoughts and feelings. They have great insights into their rationalizations, their psychological defenses, their coping mechanisms, their infantile fixations, and such. They need to pay more attention to what they do. In doing what is purposeful and proper to the varied situations of life, they find that they have less need for elaborate theories of the mind. They discover that much of their intellectual theorizing had been used as an escape from responsible, attentive living. They need to get on about paying their debts to the world.

Morita pointed out that our intellectual understanding and our feelings don't always match one another neatly. We may know that we won't smash the valuable pot we hold in our hands, but we still feel fear that we might do so. We might feel uncomfortable looking down from a height, all the while knowing that we are being very careful not to lose our balance. We may know that this particular snake or insect is harmless and yet feel revulsion and terror while handling the creature. We may realize that the celebrity in front of us is just another human but feel awed and nervous all the same. As we act in the world we learn about these conflicts and contradictions. We come to accept them as natural aspects of our psychological functioning. In the acceptance, we find they have less power over us. Because these contradictions are part of us, by accepting them we are accepting ourselves. This hang-up is just another aspect of me, and I am just another aspect of this Reality in this Moment. It's all quite natural. Now, what needs to be done next? And we get on about living.

Some of my students complain that they feel no gratitude toward their work. They can find nothing interesting about working in general. They would prefer to pass their days gently in idleness. Yet they feel some vague discomfort, as though they should be feeling more productive, they should be making more of a contribution to the world. For most of us, sitting and thinking about work is no fun. The way we develop an interest in some aspect of Reality, work included, is by acting on it. So we must be careful about the activities in which we engage. Our interests will follow along in the directions of our activities. As for work, our interest in some task has the opportunity to grow when we undertake the task. Work may become more interesting when we find new ways to do it. It is foolishness to wait for interest and gratitude toward work to grow as we sit on the couch watching television. Performing our tasks develops interest in them.

Similarly, we outgrow our narrow self-doubts and anxieties by leaving them alone as we go on about living well. We grow accustomed to our shyness and self-criticism and find such traits diminishing as we exert effort in our activities and succeed. We may even come to feel gratitude toward our neurotic past-selves because they prodded us to discover this wonderful lifeway. We become adaptable, flexible, natural, truly alive.

Thankfulness is a natural consequence of this process. As we shift from self-focus to Reality-focus we recognize what Reality is presenting to us. Our actions become purpose-filled with concrete, specific deeds of repayment. We see ourselves no longer standing apart from Reality, demanding our proper share, but as part of Reality, benefited and benefiting others.

The Perfect Mate

There is nothing wrong with going for the best, unless perfectionism and ideals interfere with doing our realistic best right now. Professor Akira Ishii tells the story of his disappointing experience with eels. When he was a child he loved to eat broiled eels, but they are a delicacy in Japan and rather expensive. So he never got his fill of eels. Then on his eleventh or twelfth birthday his family treated him to all the eels he could eat. How wonderful! He ate his fill. But thereafter he compared the few skimpy eels served to him in restaurants with the feast he had eaten as a youth. How disappointing! Then, one evening he was served eels that were so delicious they made him forget how few there were. Unfortunately, after that meal he kept comparing the flavor of the eels served to him in ordinary restaurants with those tasty eels of the past. Again, he was disappointed. At last he came to realize that the eel on the plate right in front of him was the best eel in the world. The disappointment generated by perfectionistic comparison disappeared.

Not a few people who come to me are disappointed with their partners. Husbands, wives, lovers, business associates, boyfriends, girlfriends, same sex or not--they all seem to be imperfect. They fail to live up to our ideals. The partner may not offer enough intellectual stimulation or passion or determination to succeed. It is noteworthy that the very trait the partner lacks becomes the most important trait possible. The positive qualities are taken for granted while the negative qualities draw attention and concern. Of course, we may have some minor imperfections, too, but at least we are working on them. Those partners don't seem to care about self-improvement.

As you know, Constructive Living never recommends ignoring reality. I would never suggest that you lie to yourself about your partner, that you pretend your partner is perfect. However, focusing only on faults is a kind of ignoring of reality, too. We don't usually find ourselves in partnerships with people who have no endearing qualities. Something attracted us to them initially. That eel in front of you is the best eel in the world for you right now. Even if you are working toward a divorce or separation or other breaking of the partnership you will find it useful to seek your partner's positive qualities and thank and praise him or her for those qualities. Yes, even while doing what needs to be done to dissolve the partnership. To do so is not hypocrisy, it is recognizing and acknowledging a part of reality you may have noticed right along or something you may have forgotten.

Life is uncertain. People come and go. When we find someone who has many of the attributes we hope for in a partner we may latch onto them and wish they had those few missing qualities. We may try to get everything we need from one person. But trying to fill even our social needs in one partner may be impossible. Relatives, friends, acquaintances, neighbors, memberships, sporting companions, and the like may be necessary.

In addition to these real social needs is a need for a reasonable attitude toward others. When my life is geared primarily toward getting my social (or any other personal) needs met there will always be dissatisfaction. When my attitude is truly geared toward seeing that my partner's (friend's, neighbor's) actions are being appreciated and their needs are being met, then there is a real chance for satisfaction. Remember, the best way to meet others' needs is not to be their obedient slave. That is mere cowardice and laziness. Finding the dignified, honorable, practical, sensible way to appreciate and serve others is a difficult and rewarding undertaking.

Again, when the emphasis is on getting my share I'll always be disappointed. When the emphasis is on realistically recognizing what I am already receiving and working to repay those around me there is the only genuine opportunity for fulfillment. Taking care of me first includes taking care of others. The two objectives aren't separate, and they certainly can't be done effectively in some serial order, one after another.

My Constructive Living Reciprocity Reflections at 35,000 Feet

As you may know, I fear to fly. And yet I've been flying for more than forty years. Within one seven-month period I flew to China, New York, Seattle, Japan, Australia, New Zealand, Miami, Washington DC, Hawaii and back to Los Angeles again. In that short period I flew on more than a half dozen airlines and types of aircraft. Flew scared. But there were people who needed to hear words about Constructive Living and people who needed to see someone who, frightened, did what he needed to do anyway. So I flew, was flying as I wrote these words at that very moment in a DC-10 over the Midwest headed for home.

Fears need not stop us from doing what is important for us to do--that is the message I have taught and lived for the past forty years. Now, in flight when even mild turbulence rattles us my hands perspire and my stomach tightens. My mind knows intellectually that all is well. I look around and see cabin crew going about their routine duties, standing and walking in the aisles. Fear isn't rational It cannot be turned off by reasoning. Fear just comes as it will, not as I will it. Now I'm reflecting on the efforts of others who are contributing to my flight. I'm held aloft here not only by those powerful DC-10 engines, but by the labor of people--many of whom I've never met. Let's begin with the ground crew that serviced and fueled this plane, the designers and testers of the aircraft, and the test pilot(s) who risked their lives to see that the plane was airworthy. My travel agent went to the trouble to book this flight so that I would have a non-stop trip to Los Angeles. At Dulles airport a pleasant lady checked me in and passed along my baggage to handlers who packed it safely aboard for me. Another kind lady answered my nervous phone call this morning to reconfirm the reservation and departure time. She ended our phone exchange with the kind wish that I "have a pleasant trip."

There is a pilot and first officer on the flight deck. Standing invisibly behind them are their instructors and others who designed and built flight instruction manuals and navigation equipment. Safety engineers built backup systems to improve my chances of arriving home safely.

The cabin crew serves my meals and otherwise distracts me from my anxiety with a film and magazines. They remind me of safety precautions and contingencies in case some problem should occur. So many people have considered my safety and have developed ways to preserve it!

Ground controllers pass my plane along from point to point so that we don't collide with other planes. They guide us to secure takeoffs and landings. How alert they remain for my safety!

You may say that all these people have been properly and amply paid for their services. I won't deny that they receive salaries in small part derived from the tickets I have purchased. But the fact remains that their efforts, their long hours and perspiration and careful thought and expertise permit me this rapid form of travel. And the money I used for the tickets, of course, wasn't mine. It was given to me by other people who kindly read my books and invited me to speak to them and agreed to publish my books. These people, too, hold me aloft in this reclining seat. As do the teachers who instructed me in the work I do, those who painstakingly taught me the Japanese language, and the parents who gave me this body and nurtured it during infancy and childhood. Thanks to those people I could make a living and thus buy the ticket that allows me to fly today.

Perhaps some of those airline employees are thinking that they are only doing a routine job; perhaps some are doing only the minimum to get their paycheck; perhaps only a few, sometimes, consider me (or the passenger whom I represent) as they go about their work. Nonetheless, the efforts of all these people keep me aloft. The result of their work keeps me flying even when their attitudes are less than ideal.

Come to think of it, my attitude is not always self-denying in service to those who count on me, either. How could I ask qualities of these tens of thousands of others when I don't exhibit those qualities at all times myself? And yet I do ask such qualities from them. Self-centered creature that I am, I denounce the self-centeredness of others.

How can I complain when the flight doesn't proceed with absolute smoothness for my convenience? When I think of the tens of thousands of people who linked hands to reach from ground level to 35,000 feet in order to keep me flying, how can I feel anything but wonder and gratitude? Yet, again, I do. I feel fear, too, and a fervent wish to arrive soon and unhurt.

Foolish and self-centered though I am my debt to my benefactors cannot be denied, mustn't be ignored. Thank you all for this flight and the ones last Thursday, and the one last week and the one before that and...

VIII. Constructive Living Maxims

Rain Maxims

Maxims are ways of using words to remind ourselves of Constructive Living principles. Language is a useful tool, albeit in some ways a dangerous one. We must often remind ourselves that words about reality aren't the reality itself.

Constructive Living is like a language. Once a language is learned it can never be totally forgotten. You can never return to a condition in which the sounds are a meaningless jumble as they were before you began your study of the language. You can never see your everyday life as you did before beginning your study of Constructive Living. Whether you are completely fluent in Constructive Living or not you retain your ability to use this view of life to make sense of your world. More than that, once you have some fundamental grasp of the principles (the grammar and vocabulary, if you like), you cannot completely set them aside for any length of time.

Constructive Living is not merely another language; Constructive Living is your native language.

There is Reality's work only you can do.

No need for perfection--Reality takes care of you anyway.

Have you been through enough to appreciate Reality when you see it?

Some people know how to fly; they must learn how to walk.

Happy birthday, Mom. Without yours I wouldn't have one. Love, Your child.

If it's raining, and you have an umbrella, use it, even if the umbrella is tattered and imperfect.

Constructive Living--when you care to do the very best.

If alcohol is your koan; solve it.

I've had lots of troubles in my life and most of them never happened. --David Miles

Run to the edge of the cliff and stop on a dime; then thank those who helped you get to the dime. --David Miles

When the seas are stormy, thank the boatmaker and keep on rowing. --Henry Kahn.

Reality never tires, only you do. --Daniel Hoppe

A Ph. Do is more useful than a Ph.D. --Rose Anderson

Reality school--where you're on scholarship even though you are flunking, but you never get to repeat a course. --Rose Anderson

Ears hear more than thoughts do. --Fred Ketchum

Come to your senses. --Deanna Kirk

Do think then thank. --Deanna Kirk

The steps to climb Mt. Everest and the steps to climb a small hill are the same size. --Robert Orenstein

Today is For-giving. --Patricia Ryan-Madson

In every moment opportunities for action.
In every action opportunities for thanks. --Robert Orenstein

Swimming Maxims

Maxims are pithy ways of citing and recalling Constructive Living principles. Here are some recent Constructive Living maxims. Most of them were created by Constructive Living instructors during their training at the ten-day certification courses around the United States. I have included a short explanation for some of them.

When you fall, thank the ground for catching you. --Crilly Butler

Don't do what needs to be not done.--Crilly Butler

It's been real. --Kate Bean (A Constructive Living greeting.)

When life throws you a curve...SWING! --Bob Brown

Reality will never tell you a lie, but I won't ask you to believe that.--Mary Ann Thomas

Food won't make you fat.--Mary Ann Thomas (Eating does.)

The present is received whatever the wrapping paper. --Diana Peterson

Poison ivy and snakes illuminate the woods. --David Pollock (They invite us to pay attention during out walks through the woods.)

Self-help books don't work. --Nicholas Callie, Jr. (People work.)

The more I look within the more I find I'm without. --Joan Fischer

Constructive Living people do it on purpose. --David Hudson and Rami Shapiro

Put off procrastination. --Shana Alexander

Act is fact.--Ron Green

Even when you give up on reality, reality never gives up on you.

Wherever you go there you are; wherever you are someone helped you get there.--Ron Green

Give yourself away; you weren't yours in the first place.--Ron Green

The ocean smooths the edges from rocks provided they stay in the ocean.

No journeys, only this step now.

With eyes on the distant mountain watch the winding path underfoot.

Purposeful action gets the job done faster than humility.

Tired of wearing old clothes? Why keep wearing them?

Your self is shrinking as your world is growing.

IX. CONSTRUCTIVE LIVING KOANS

Koans

Koans are about making mental leaps. The koan practice helps train the mind to find certain kinds of essences in everyday life. If these essences are pointed out to the student they may be appreciated, but to explain them outright gives the student no chance to make the mental leap alone. To explain a koan to a student would be rather like reading a book of chess problems while consulting the answer pages instead of working out the answers without help. The doing itself produces some skill and persistence.

Koans are puzzles that keep the mind occupied, teaching basic principles in novel ways. It is best to ponder Constructive Living koans over a span of time, one at a time. When one puzzle is mastered or when you are blocked after a couple of weeks working on a Constructive Living koan move along to the next one. A well-constructed (well-discovered) koan has layers of meaning. Below I have written some koans in prose and some in poetic form. Answers can be confirmed by certified Constructive Living instructors. Answers are right or wrong and do not depend on the subjective evaluation of the student. An answer that begins, "For me, the meaning of this koan is..." is invariably wrong.

The unknown

A young man keeps sending postcards to his far away lover as he travels. He is unaware that his lover has written to his home informing him that she is leaving him for another. He won't get her letter until he returns months later from his extended trip. Were his postcards written for nothing?

The lemon meringue pie koan

The first of three men enters a room, walks over to a chair with a lemon meringue pie on it and sits down on the pie. After a time the second man enters the room saying, "I don't like what I am about to do, but I can't seem to help myself from doing it. Furthermore I do understand some of the underlying reasons for this act." Then he, too, walks over to the chair and sits on a lemon meringue pie. The third fellow, after sitting on a lemon meringue pie, rises to say "What an uncomfortable yet vital lesson I have learned from this experience." Then he proceeds to sit on yet another lemon meringue pie. What is the difference among these men? What is the similarity?

Eat, sleep

What Constructive Living sense can we make of Zen psychology's advice to "Eat when hungry; sleep when tired"? The Zen maxim cannot have the transparent meaning it appears to have. Imagine a visitor comes for dinner and there isn't enough food for visitor and family. Because one is hungry should one ignore the visitor's needs or convenience and eat anyway?

One sort of Constructive Living sense we can make of the advice to "Eat when hungry; sleep when tired" is that there is no need to look for deep hidden complex motivations underlying simple acts. Such concerns with complex searches simply distract us from doing what needs doing. Can you find other Constructive Living interpretations in this maxim?

Assorted brief koans
1. What is wrong and right about throwing leftovers from the refrigerator and not finishing all the food on one's plate as methods of losing weight? What strategies can you suggest as better? What broader meaning can you find in this koan?

2. How am I getting along with my dishes? What is the purpose of developing intimacy with things as well as people?

3. Discover the meaning underlying these words written by Ron Green:
     "The whole world is living us. This chair is doing its chairness, aside from my opinions and notions about it. It is alive in its chairness. If one puts aside one's self and sees what is--there is just reality.   The self we think we are is a non-self made up of all the selves in the universe."

X. Constructive Living Tales

Most of these tales were written for particular students. Each tale carries one or more Constructive Living points I wished to convey to someone. Reading about a character in a story gives my students a distanced perspective that allows them to see themselves more clearly.

Diamond Misery

Once upon a puzzling time people evaluated the value of their contacts with others in terms of how much they suffered when those contacts ended. When Floppy's boyfriend broke up with her she was certain that he hadn't been very important to her because she didn't feel terribly terrible. When Floppy's brother, Flippy, faced the death of his Aunt Val, he didn't grieve much, so he decided that he hadn't been close to his Aunt. All that seemed to make some sense.

Then, when Floppy's father died and she was sad but not all broken up, Floppy didn't know what to think. She *had* been close to her father. Nevertheless, she seemed to be able to go about her daily life without collapsing, and she only cried once. Others wondered why she didn't hurt more. Floppy herself wondered. Had there been some hidden grudge against her father? Was she stunted emotionally in some way to be unable to recognize and express her overwhelming grief?

Floppy's mother was upset with her for not falling apart. Her social world certainly expected more tears. Perhaps they considered her a cold, unfeeling bitch, or so Floppy worried.

It wasn't that Floppy was fighting against her grief. She welcomed it; she wanted more of it. Thus, she could confirm her deep love for her father. But feelings are intransigent critters--they don't go away when we want them to, and they don't appear on cue either.

Floppy found herself pressured to fake more misery than she really felt. Then she got confused about which was real and which was artifice. Then she got confused about who was feeling this mixed bag of feelings.

After a long time, Floppy figured out that it makes more sense to value folks while you are with them than to try to compute their worth to you after they are gone. And the grieving comes when it will.

This story includes the restatement of a familiar theme--feelings are uncontrollable directly by the will. They are best accepted as they are. They provide information, but they are not the measure of our lives.

Runaway

Lisa Squirrel twitched her bushy tail in the air a couple of times and raced in a series of small m's for the nearest pine tree. The velvet mountain heat didn't bother her. She loved the shadow wind that breathed caresses through her fur. Above there was only vibrating needles and rolling whiteness.

But Lisa Squirrel wasn't appreciating her forest home today. She faced a pine-sized problem. She sat on a branch high up and watched the scrub oaks across the way overflow and dribble down the mountain. Her eyes followed suit, overflowing with warm tears. Her male friend, Ricky Squirrel was showing signs of losing interest. And the only solution Lisa could come up with was to dump him before he got around to dumping her. He was a bit slow for Lisa, anyway, and his eyes wandered too much. Still, she would miss him.

On the Angeles Crest Highway nearby huge trucks lumbered past like obese matrons heading for another cocktail. Harold pulled his car from the end of the parade onto a turnout and exited. The world seemed to be sliding past at 45 miles per hour. He felt that he skated rather than walked away from the car. Exhaustion forced his eyelids open. They would no longer close, yet he felt himself slipping into sleep with eyes wide open. Sleep, he realized, is a state of giving up one's mind. It has nothing to do with the body at all, he thought.

Harold was moving on to (hopefully) better things before the boss back in Pasadena realized that he had given Harold too much responsibility on the job. Harold had maneuvered a transfer through the main office. Denver would be a welcome change. Southern California was due to fall into the ocean anyway, wasn't it? He leaned back against the trunk of a pine and dozed.

Overhead the United flight to Newark carried Clara back to Mom and Dad. Five months of college had been enough. Bill was a nice guy, but being around him was like being fed by an ant. No matter what its will and effort might be, the results are insufficient. Better to bail out before the loneliness deepened in that arid land so far away from home.

Who knows what might happen?

In life you have to break in your own shoes. Some people try to do that by running away.

Being Ordinary

Once upon an urban time there was a spiritual master who watched video, ate frozen foods, and drove a pickup truck. Very few people recognized him as a spiritual master because he wore no robes, he ate meat, and he was constantly tinkering with a straight-eight engine that resisted efforts to keep it running. What business would a spiritual master have with grease all over his hands?

A few kids in the neighborhood recognized that there was something special about Hank. (His name was another liability in the spiritual circus circuit--not exotic at all.) He didn't swear when he dropped the hammer on his foot; he just picked it up and went back to pounding. He explained what he was repairing to even the greenest young mechanic. His garage workshop seemed tidier than most. And the only time the kids ever saw him in a rush was when a grinder motor caught fire, and then he had the extinguisher chemical all over it before anyone had time to get scared.

Kids noticed that people came by to visit Hank every now and then. A few wore fancy suits and looked like insurance company executives or bankers. Most, however, dressed simply, perhaps a bit on the drab side, or so it looked to the youngsters. Hank would stop what he was doing--watering or working on the truck or patching up the house or digging in the garden or lounging in the hammock--and he and his visitor would disappear in the house for an hour or two. Then they would come out and shake hands and Hank would stand and watch the visitors drive off until they were out of sight. Then he would just pick up right where he left off.

Another peculiarity about Hank was that he would stop what he was doing and listen to whatever any kid had to say about anything for as long as the kid wanted to talk. Now that kind of adult is as rare as they come. New kids in the neighborhood seemed starved for such attention. They took advantage of Hank's listening ears for what seemed to them long periods of time. And Hank never seemed to tire of listening and asking questions. But there were baseball games and trap-door spiders and skateboards calling. In time the new kids, too, came around only when then had something they thought important enough to ask or tell Hank.

No temple, no beard, no mystical symbols. There was a television antenna on the roof and empty frozen dinner containers in his trash sometimes. Admittedly, Hank did wear sandals on hot summer days. To the kids and (apparently) to the visitors Hank was a special person. To the parents of the young people in the neighborhood, Hank was a nice guy, an ordinary guy. He wasn't particularly wealthy or famous or successful; certainly, he was no saint. After all...

Constructive Living provides a life strategy for becoming ordinary. We fear that we are not ordinary (neurotic) and we yearn to be not ordinary (superior). Constructive Living teaches us how to be natural, just ourselves, nothing special. Disappointed? You expected more? Perhaps there is consolation in the truth that being nothing special, in the sense used here, is a state both rewarding and difficult to achieve.

For the marvel, the special quality, is in this moment, in this unique circumstance, not in you or me. I am just a part of this moment, an aspect, a participant. I am just ordinary, but this Reality is ever-changing wonder!

Sleeping Sickness

Once upon a time there was a land in which the people thought that by sleeping with each other they could get their partners' magical powers and avoid loneliness.

They were wrong.

This is the shortest of the stories I have written for my students. It was written for a person who used seduction to bring about temporary feelings of security and to hide from gnawing loneliness. We discussed alternative activities to achieve more controllable, long-term goals.

Royalty

Once upon a time there was a prince who liked being just a prince. He knew that someday his father would step down and he would ascend to the throne, but he dreaded that day.

"I am a mere prince, Father. I have many sisters. Let one of them rule the land."

"The people expect you to rule them, my son. Why do you struggle with your destiny?"

"I am a very good prince," the young man answered. "I am skilled at doing princely things. I can hold my own in combat, woo pretty maidens, dance until dawn, and drink and ride my stallion with the best of them. But I am not a king. A king must be serious and wise and just. Kings know much more than I do. I cannot be a king."

The royal monarch only laughed.

Now it happened that later that year the ruler of the land fell ill. The illness lingered for months. It was rumored that the king was about to turn over power to his son.

The prince began to panic. "I'm not ready for this," he cried. "Can someone else take over for a few years? How about a council of governors? If only Mother hadn't died... I wish that a queen could rule the land. Oh, dear me, what shall I do?"

Two days before the coronation ceremony all the palace was in an uproar. The prince had locked himself in his room, and he refused to come out. Upon hearing this tragic news, the king immediately called the grand wizard to his sickbed. He looked the old man straight in the eye and told him to take care of the problem. The grand wizard nodded and left with a swirl of his robes. He knew exactly what to do. For hadn't a very similar event occurred forty years before, as the current monarch ascended the throne?

The grand wizard knocked on the prince's door. He carried a tray of food in his left hand.

"Go away," a voice called from inside the room.

"Sire, I have your meal tray."

"I don't want anything to eat. Go away!"

"But, Sire, I have the dynastic pill for you to take with your meal."

"The dynastic pill?" The voice sounded somewhat closer to the door.

"Of course, it is the medicine that makes you a ruler." The voice of the grand wizard was scarcely a whisper now. "You cannot reign without taking the dynastic pill."

"'I never heard of such a thing."

"And please, Sire, do not tell anyone else about it," whispered the old man. "If word got out, many would desire to take the pill and become a monarch."

Curiosity and hope filled the young man. He opened the door a crack and peeked out into the hall.

"Come in, quickly!"

The grand wizard scurried into the prince's chambers, tray in hand.

"All right, where is the pill?" demanded the prince.

"It is inside the bottle there in the center of your tray. You had best read the label and instructions carefully before taking it."

"You may go now." The prince turned away and sat on the bed with the magic bottle in his hand.

"Yes, Sire." And the grand wizard left the room.

The prince eagerly read the label on the bottle. It read: "Dynastic pill. Prepared personally by each monarch for his royal successor. Read the instructions inside carefully."

The prince pulled the glass stopper from the bottle and peered inside. A sheet of paper and one large white pill greeted his eye.

The sheet of paper must contain the instructions, he thought. As he began to unfurl it, his imagination turned toward the coronation banquet. In his mind's eye he pictured himself standing regally at the table head, toasting the kingdom. Poised, confident, fully a king...

Two days later the coronation took place without incident. The court was buzzing about the fine bearing of the new king. The common folk rejoiced at the prospect of another in a long line of wise and charismatic monarchs.

Oh yes, about the pill. As the prince's trembling fingers unfolded the instructions, he recognized his father's handwriting:

For you, my son,

No man is ever ready for such authority as this. No man begins by feeling like a king. You become a king by being one. In time, you will wear your crown as comfortably as anyone has.

There is no magic in this pill. It is made of the bitterest herbs. The instructions are to hold it in your mouth until you grow used to the bitterness. Then, when you have conquered it, when the pill has completely dissolved, you may swallow it. That is all.

Your loving father

Sometimes we do not feel confident to do the tasks that life brings us to do. Other people appear to be confident as they do their tasks. We want a magic pill (or an education, or a secure job, or a fine spouse, or much money, or something else) to give us confidence. But confidence comes after we have done our work and succeeded, not before. It is natural to lack confidence before starting a new school subject or moving into marriage or taking on new responsibilities at work. Accept the bitter taste of self-doubt while going about mastering the situation.

Stoptime

Little Suzy was in kindergarten. One day she brought a pumpkin seed home from class. Her homework assignment was to plant the seed and water it and grow a pumpkin for next Halloween.

She packed rich, black soil into a glass jar, planted her seed, watered it carefully, and set it on the kitchen window shelf. Then she sat down to watch the seed grow.

"What are you doing, Suzy?" her teen-aged sister, Lucy, asked.

"I'm waiting for the pumpkin to grow so that I can put it in a larger jar," Suzy replied.

"Silly," Lucy laughed. "It will take a long time before that pumpkin comes up."

"That's all right; I'll wait. What are you doing sitting by the phone?"

"I'm hoping Bill will call me. He's that cute new guy at school. I think he likes me."

"Does he know our phone number?" Suzy asked a sensible question.

"Hmmm. Maybe. He knows Bob, and Bob knows it."

Just then their father entered the kitchen.

"Any telephone calls for me, Lucy?" he asked.

"No, not this morning. Anything special?"

"Well, I sent that manuscript off to the publisher's last week. They should let me know soon if they want to publish it or not."

"Well, nothing so far."

"Thanks, I'd better get back to that lawnmower." He grabbed a can of beer from the refrigerator and went back out through the screen door.

From the next room Lucy's mother's voice could barely be heard above the whir of the sewing machine. She was talking to herself.

"When will that man come to his senses about the writing business? He could be making a good, steady living as an engineer. I've waited sixteen years for the light to dawn on him that he'll never make it as an author. If it weren't for my sewing and his parents' money...

The cat scratched at the screen door. Suzy ran to let it in. Tail in the air, her chubby pet headed for the cupboard where the cat food was kept. It sat and scratched and whined in its cat's voice, waiting to be fed.

This story seems to be getting nowhere, the author thought. Perhaps tomorrow I'll think of an inspiring ending.

In this story everyone is waiting for something. Suzy is waiting for the pumpkin seed to grow; Lucy is waiting for a telephone call; the cat is waiting to be fed; even the author is waiting to finish the story. Some people seem to turn their lives off as they wait for something. In other words, they only wait and do not use their time wisely while waiting. When my younger students are waiting to learn the results of entrance examinations, when they are waiting for their bus to arrive, when they are waiting for a friend to telephone, what do they do? Life seems very long to young people, but it is too short to waste even a minute. Young or old, we recommend to our students that they fill their waiting moments with fun and study and other activity. One of our Constructive Living action maxims is, "Don't put your life on hold."

A Boy and His Cat

There was once a little boy with a pet cat. He kept the cat in a wire cage all of the time. Even when he fed the cat and when he petted it, he never took the animal from its cage.

"You can't trust cats," he said. "They will run away if you give them a chance."

"But don't you love your cat?" his friend asked him.

"Not particularly," he replied. "But it's mine, and it's not going to get away." His mother argued that since he fed the cat and stroked its furry body, the pet would want to stay nearby. But he didn't want to take any chances.

His father felt sorry for the cat and threatened to put his son in a cage so he could see what it felt like to be cooped up all the time. But the boy knew that his father was only bluffing.

Month after month passed, and the cat's restlessness turned to lethargy. The pacing stopped and the animal lay curled in a corner of the small cage day after day, refusing to eat.

"Your cat will die," his mother warned.

"Let the cat out," his father ordered.

"It's only trying to make me take it out of the cage," cried the boy, and he threw a tantrum.

So the cat stayed as it was until one day it died.

"I don't care if I take it out now," he said calmly, and he turned the cage on end and dumped the stiff, furry body into the trash.

"It never got out until I was ready."

The main theme of this story concerns possessiveness. What is the relationship between love and control? This tale is useful for some troubled marriages and other relationships. As in all these fables there are subthemes that can be useful for certain sorts of clients. What does my student see as the proper child-rearing functions of parents? What part does the cat play in the permanent caging?

One Step Forward, Two Steps Back

Sir Jules was a knight with a grand goal in life. He intended someday to climb the highest mountain in the kingdom of Uckland. His family was proud of Sir Jules' ambition. They looked forward to the day his purpose would be accomplished.

Despite his youth Sir Jules was not an impetuous or foolhardy knight. Very prudently he decided that there was no sense rushing headlong into a mountain-climbing expedition without proper training and preparation. Perhaps, he thought, it would be wiser to start with smaller mountains and work up to the challenge of Mount Summit. So he tried climbing the much smaller Mount Norep.

Part of the way up during the ascent of Mount Norep, Sir Jules became winded. His calves and shoulders ached from the strain of climbing. Being a prudent fellow, he decided that it would be dangerous to overexert himself so early in his climbing career. He turned around and went home for more training.

Months later he began the ascent of Mount Norep once again. This time he carried a lighter pack and wore special supportive shoes. But surprisingly, he found himself winded even earlier than before. His heart began pounding with the exertion. No use risking some sort of heart attack, he reflected reasonably as he sat on a boulder by the side of the trail. I'll try this practice climb another time when I am in better condition.

There were several moderate-sized hills not too far from the castle. For several weeks Sir Jules carried his pack to these hills and hiked through them. After a while, he had his servant carry the pack as far as the hills. Then he hefted the pack and began climbing. After all, he reasoned, he needn't exert himself on the flat road leading to the hills; he was in training for climbing only. But walking about in the hills became boring. What interested the young knight was a steeper climb. Still, he didn't feel quite ready to tackle Mount Norep yet.

The castle walls were, of course, vertical masses of assembled rock. You can't find anything steeper than vertical, thought Sir Jules. He abandoned his hikes in the hills in order to practice scaling the castle walls with rope and spiked boots. Unfortunately, he soon discovered that he was afraid of heights, at least the sheer heights of castle walls. So, being a cautious person, he abandoned that method of training.

If I plan my ascent more carefully in order to avoid the steeper and more demanding paths up Mount Summit, he considered reasonably, the expedition will surely go more smoothly. No one would argue with such a sensible course of action. So the young knight worked in his room around the clock poring over maps of the various approaches to the summit.

But as the weeks passed he seemed to grow pale and weak. Day and night he spent in his castle room planning and imagining and wishing for the success of his project. Strangely, each day the mountain seemed higher in his imagination.

In time, people began to wonder if he was really serious about his plan. After all, what he did was merely to sit in his room and talk about what he hoped to do someday. The plans became more and more vague. The date of the expedition became some distant future time when he felt more ready to conquer the mountain.

The mountain won its battle with Sir Jules because the mountain just sat there and so did Sir Jules. Mountains don't have to put one tired, trembling foot before the other in order to achieve success; humans do.

On the surface, Sir Jules's thinking may appear circumspect and rational. Yet this sort of thinking kept him retreating from necessary action. It is common in bright people with neurotic tendencies. Such thinking is neurotic.

The Unicorn and the Menicorn

Where the unicorn has a horn projecting out into the world, the menicorn has a sort of deep pimple, called an introhorn. The unicorn uses its horn to touch things, rather as we use our fingers. The horn is quite sensitive, so the unicorn can learn a lot about a tree or a person just by brushing against it with its horn. The horn is so sensitive that sometimes the unicorn gets hurt-when it nudges something with thorns, for example, or when it bumps against something hard. Still, the unicorn uses its horn quite a lot in its daily life. It is a useful sensory organ.

The menicorn, on the other hand, has its very sensitive dimpled introhorn. But because the introhorn projects inward instead of outward, the menicorn doesn't use it to explore its surroundings. Instead, it grazes passively hoping the wind would blow something into its concave sense organ. The menicorn often wishes that something interesting would fall into its introhorn. Most of the time, however, what falls into the menicorn's introhorn comes from the menicorn itself. Naturally, when it sweats or cries the salt water collects in the introhorn. Strands from its mane and flakes of skin drift into the introhorn, as well. Over the years, the menicorn becomes exceedingly familiar with these aspects of itself. It longs for new stimulation from outside, but it doesn't know how to go searching for new experiences. So the menicorn lives with the overly familiar every day and grows more discontent year by year.

What the typical menicorn doesn't know is that it can reverse the growth of its introhorn and get it to project outward like the horn of a unicorn. It never occurs to most menicorns that they will ever be anything but passive recipients of what the wind and gravity bring their way.

A few menicorns have made the transition. It takes getting out of the pasture and into the woods with all those poking, jabbing twigs and branches. The introhorn gets irritated by all the contact with the bristly underbrush, and it begins to swell. The painful swelling grows outward and, in time, becomes toughened. A menicorn can learn to control the growth of its horn by choosing where to poke it.

You will find that the unicorns with the longest and finest horns were once menicorns; though some of them have forgotten.

This story is for self-centered, introverted students. It provides the occasion to talk about what they envy in others, the pain of exploration, and the rewards of getting involved in their surroundings.

The Doll Carriage

Renee is in her late twenties now, a pretty girl with good posture and appropriately crossed ankles and studied grace. She is bent on finding a doll carriage. Some would call her quest an obsession. Every weekend she can be found rummaging around in the huge attic of the Victorian house in which she lives searching for an old doll carriage.

Her story begins nearly twenty years ago. Her mother asked Renee to put away the lovely new doll carriage (it was a Christmas gift from both her parents) and help set the table. After the table was set there were other chores to do. Her father left them that evening after dinner; her mother lost interest in living. So it fell to Renee to take care of her mother, her brothers and sisters.

There wasn't much time to play with her dolls in the following days. Being a practical girl she packed away her doll carriage, collapsing it and returning it to its original container, storing it in the attic. And she waited for a better time. During the passing years there was so much to do. Her mother stumbled her way out of depression's fog. Her brothers finished their education. One sister got married. They all appreciated Renee's sacrifices for them. She had been so careful not to cause anyone trouble. There had been slips here and there, but, overall, Renee had been a model child.

Renee was about twenty-six when she felt the urge to find the old doll carriage packed away for all these years. Her brother noticed that she was in the attic shoving around the trunks and boxes. He wondered what she was about, noticed her empty hands as she descended the attic stairs several hours later.

"What were you doing up there?" he asked in that challenging tone so characteristic of his voice and his life.

"Nothing," Renee replied absently. "just looking for something."

But the next weekend Renee was back in the attic again, and the next, and the next. Always she looked for the doll carriage.

After several months her mother offered to help her search for whatever it was she was looking for. But Renee wanted to do it without assistance from anyone else.

The strange thing was that Renee had absolutely no idea what she wanted to do with the doll carriage if she ever found it. Surely, she had no serious prospects of marriage, didn't feel prepared to have a child of her own. Anyway, the carriage was too small for a full-sized infant. It was completely useless to her, yet she felt impelled to find it.

Some days she searched methodically; some days she flung boxes frantically all over the attic. What could have happened to her childhood plaything? Surely it was here, somewhere in the attic. Perhaps it was hidden under the gowns she had sewn during her teen years. Perhaps it lay beneath the old textbooks from the days when she had finally escaped to a small college up North.

At last, late in her twenty-eighth year, Renee gave up. She sat on the attic floor and cried until there were no more tears to stir the dust next to her hand. She grieved for all that she'd never had and could never go back to find.

Then she went out and found a job that helped kids be kids while they had the chance.

This story was written for someone who seemed to have missed her childhood and was searching for it again. More and more I encounter among my students histories of children who were forced by circumstances to be supportive and adultlike during childhood. Too many had to be like parents to their biological parents. Of course, children should be allowed to be children. But what can be done by those who weren't allowed their childhood when they were young? Renee found a solution.

Junkies

In the mythical land of Dok there was a winged horse, Satori, upon which only a brave few had ever ridden. Those who rode upon this winged wonder appeared to be changed in some marvelous way. So it is no wonder that many desired to mount Satori.

How-to books concerned with tracking down the steed, gaining its confidence, and leaping astride its broad back were long sellers in the marketplace. And, of course, those who claimed to have ridden Satori could find an audience whenever they spoke.

Some of the fine citizens of Dok were what might be called "wing junkies." They bought every book about flying on Satori, took courses on mounting, attended lectures by famous riders, collected paintings and recordings of odd music that were supposed to be related to Satori.

These wing junkies had difficulty distinguishing what was genuine from what was fake. Anyone who used fashionable words and acted humble-superior could attract their attention and their money. In fact, for many of them, the goal of riding Satori had long ago given way to the goal of just thinking about riding it. The idea of the winged horse was so attractive that it was sufficient for these wing junkies.

There evolved a sort of informal club among the wing junkies of Dok. They saw each other at this academic lecture and at that bareback workshop. They exchanged clever words and techniques. They all considered themselves to be preparing for their big day with the heavenly steed, but, strangely, none of them actually rode it.

Over the years, a very few of the wing junkies dropped out of the chic movement. They gave up reading about the methods order to try one of them--not for a weekend, but for a lifetime. Within a year or so, these dropouts discovered that what they thought they knew about galloping through the heavens was no more substantial than clouds. Their preparations took a new turn. Sticking to one method of riding wasn't nearly as much fun tripping off to this "ashranch" and that communal corral. It took diligent effort and constant attention. Even then, some dropouts never found Satori, and some who found the horse never climbed aboard for their ride in the sky.

Even though witnessing the failure and difficulties around them, these dropouts knew in some mysterious way that they were closer to riding the stallion than when they had been wing junkies. They didn't understand how they knew this important truth, nor did they care. But the more they worked on the single method of riding, the closer they came to their goal.

Even fewer of these dropouts came to see the importance cleaning stables and oiling saddles and practicing mounting leaps whether they ever rode the winged steed or not. Some folks saw these mundane dropouts and said that they were no different from the wing junkies. Both the stable sweepers and the wing junkie were "doing their thing." Neither would be likely to ride Satori. Both were satisfied with their preparations for riding.

But wing junkies and stable sweepers aren't the same at all. Stable sweepers no longer need to ride Satori. If the horse wanders through their stables they'll climb aboard, of course. But there is a great deal of satisfaction in keeping the stables shipshape.

The wing junkies, on the other hand, need Satori because their current life is unsatisfying. And they are likely to be forever frustrated, frantically flitting from equestrian tutor to cowboy guru.

In the land of Dok few fly the skies with Satori. Yet a few have learned to walk the ground with winged feet.

The Magic Medallion

The adventurers sat hunched around a smoky fire in a hostile jungle. Each day brought them closer to their prize.

Mountains, deserts, oceans, and now a jungle--but nothing would stop them. Natives emerged from the green curtain to advise them to go back. With one hand on their rifles they continued to eat from the tin plates propped on their knees.

They sought the magic medallion, source of great power. Power would bring them riches and lives of ease. So now they suffered this miserable, dangerous existence. The crumpled map in their leader's pocket traced an unclear path toward an uncertain destination. But they could feel the closeness of the medallion. It beckoned them to future fortune. Right now, the mosquitoes feasted and the fire ants stung, but if only they could gain the prize, all would be well.

After feats of daring and close escapes and long hours of boredom and weariness they stood before the Cave of the Magic Medallion. Cautiously they entered; who knew what final menace awaited them? Their flashlights crisscrossed back and forth on the walls of the shallow, manmade hole in the hillside.

The altar stood against the back wall. They approached it. Trapdoors? Deadfalls? Nothing. And on the altar, too, nothing.

"Oh, no," they exclaimed, "someone has beaten us to the medallion."

And then they read the inscription carved below the altar. It read: "Foolish ones! Why do you seek magic power like little children lost in a fairy tale? Are you not adults? Did you not suffer and struggle to reach this place? You who succeeded in your quest have no need of magic powers. Go back and use the powers that are rightfully yours."

One of the adventurers returned home disappointed; he began to plan more expeditions, successful ones that would lead him to real treasure, not empty advice. A second member of the party picked up a few shiny pebbles near the altar. She hoped that they might have picked up some of the magical power of the medallion before it was stolen. An exhausted man ran screaming into the jungle and was never heard from again. But a handful of adventurers went home pondering the meaning of the inscription. What powers were rightfully theirs? Why should they have no need of wonderful magic? Had their expedition succeeded or not?

Water World

Once upon a fragile time people lived on the surface of a huge body of water. They walked on a thin film that covered the water's great depths. Sometimes the surface tension weakened in spots and someone began to sink. Those around the sinking person risked breaching the surface tension in order to rescue him or her. It was the custom. Such self-sacrifice was necessary in that world. When the rescuers were in danger they, too, could expect help.

Sometimes, as the tear in the surface film spread, there were whole chains of people lending a hand to their fellows. In that risky world it was good to know that supporting hands were ready to help when needed.

Nearby, another group of people lived on a small island. They were proud that each of them walked by the individual's own strength with no help or support from others. In other ways they were a very bright people. Yet because of their pride they were confined to their island. And they knew a chilly loneliness that their water-borne cousins never felt.

One of the part-truths in American culture is the part-myth of the self-made individual. That notion has both stimulated us and limited us. The other side of that truth is that we are all dependent on others for our successes and for our moment-by-moment existence. The reciprocity-inspired elements of Constructive Living assist us in recognizing this truth about mutual dependency.

Smarts

Once upon a wishful time pocket-sized dragons roamed the land. They attacked humans at will. They attacked anything in sight. Their bites rarely killed, but they were painful and took time to heal. People walked about with scars.

A philosopher arose who claimed that getting to know the dragons would cause them to cease their attacks. He and his followers made great efforts to understand and communicate with the miniature dragons. As a result, they suffered many bites, but they gathered much information about the dragons' habits.

Unfortunately, the philosopher was wrong. Knowing a lot about dragons didn't stop them from attacking. The people felt despair. Some tried to appease the dragons with every kind of personal gift and sacrifice imaginable. But giving in to the dragons seemed to be just as ineffective. In fact, sacrificing their material possessions to try to keep the dragons at bay proved more costly than enduring the occasional bite. What could they do? The people were at a loss.

All sorts of methods proved unworkable. Heavy armor restricted the wearer's movements. Flight to the mountains and beaches demonstrated only that dragons existed in those places, too. Prayers didn't destroy the dragon demons.

In time, the people learned to live with occasional pain. They avoided areas heavily infested with dragons. They kept their eyes open to avoid stepping into the path of a dragon. But they learned to go about their daily lives wearing a bandage here and there. Often, they were so involved in their work or play that they forgot about the pain, the bandages, the dragons. Such was the nature of the country.

Psychological insight doesn't erase pain or prevent its reoccurrence. It may help us spot potential trouble areas. Though we avoid what is avoidable, we cannot escape from hurt altogether. We live alongside it; we live within it; we live it. And the way we live in spite of our pain is a measure of our character.

I am told that in the dragon-infested country introduced above some people actually befriended and even married particularly large dragons. And, despite differences in their temperaments, they seem to have gotten along together pretty well.

Fluff

This is a story about cloud people. Cloud people float in the sky on word clouds. They drift mindlessly on soft pink syllables.

Large cumulus clouds are composed of words like "mystery unfolding in you," "you are God in action," "give yourself permission to be in that special magical inner place," "there is beauty and joy in everything," "celebrate yourself," "you are the Star," "you deserve a wonderful life," "it is your right as God," "you can create anything," "be a gift to the world," "allow the child in you to emerge and demonstrate your beauty and wonderment." Scattered cirrus clouds are made up of words like " effortless," "centered," "trusting," "wondrous," "magical," "wisdom," "healthy," "successful," "perfect," "love," "abundance," "transform," "energy," "whole," "complete," "perfection," "peace," "joy." The clouds offer an attractive formation sailing through the sky. But they have no substance up there in the ether.

Hiking is more difficult than sailing on clouds. It isn't nearly as much fun to weave one's way on foot through jungles and prairies as it is to drift in the sun. Climbing a mountain is hard work.

But clouds don't sail their riders over mountains, they rain.

Cloud people know that they aren't anchored to reality. They must know it. Reality keeps reminding them. Still they make effort to suspend their disbelief. They call to one another from their vaporous mounts that thinking so makes it so. They encourage others to float up for a ride in the sky. They demonstrate to us the capacity of humans to desperately believe.

Yet thunder and lightning are as real as love. And a shelter built with one's hands offers more protection in a storm than a shelter imaged and affirmed from a celestial perch.

Hazards of Brilliance

Once upon a changing time, there lived a street-wise fellow who knew the ropes of therapy, too. Let's call him Jaime. Jaime was a quick-witted fellow who knew himself through and through. He knew the games he played with himself and others. He knew intimately his strengths and weaknesses. He knew his unlimited potential.

Jaime wanted to go hiking in the mountains, but he never did. He knew the mental obstacles he threw up to impede his accomplishing his goal. He recognized the mental chatter about the hassle of getting equipment together, the difficulty of assuring comfort and safety on a mountain trail, the problem of being in less than ideal physical condition, and so on. He knew he could get out on the trail in spite of his mental vacillation.

Sometimes Jaime would sit back in a favorite recliner in his den and smile at himself and his foolishness. What an intricate and devious mind he had! But he was aware of all its tricks. He could identify each gambit, each ploy. How well he knew himself, sitting there in the recliner.

One day Jaime opened a book about Constructive Living and read the following passage: "Some very clever people have trouble grasping the essence of Constructive Living. They have been so successful at figuring things out that they overlook the simple action-orientation of this lifeway. They have become so good at seeing through their own life games that they think the seeing alone is sufficient. They are insightful and stuck in their sagacity. Too much dependence on the intellect and an obsession with insight can actually interfere with the experiential understanding of this lifeway."

Jaime closed the book, smiled, and understood exactly what the passage meant. Then he closed his eyes and drifted off to sleep.

The Slippery Throat

Once upon a time there was a little girl, Phyllis, with a slippery throat. Words slipped out of her throat so rapidly that sometimes she was surprised at what she said. Someone had told her that people didn't like little girls who are wishy-washy, so no matter how strange the words that slipped from her throat she never took them back. She stood by her words no matter what. Everyone around her thought she was very bright because her words came out so quickly; no one ever suspected her of lying because she didn't have time to make up any falsehood-- her replies came too quickly for that. And Phyllis hated to make people wait for her answers to their questions. Furthermore, in some families if you don't get your words in quickly somebody else will jump in the conversation with theirs. A slippery throat has some advantages.

Unfortunately, sometimes the words that flew from the little girl's lips weren't the words she would have liked to say. Sometimes they were even wrong. But words won't slide back down the throat easily; they can't be swallowed at all. What to do?

Sometimes Phyllis pretended she was a wall and couldn't hear or speak at all. But that was no fun and people knew better. Sometimes Phyllis put lots of food in her mouth so she wouldn't have to speak--good girls don't speak with their mouths full, you know.

As Phyllis grew up she learned to give word-package presents to others. She learned to wrap up her word gifts in just the right wrappings before offering them. It took a little more time to make them presentable, but when they slipped from her throat they fit the occasion beautifully. What a gift!

By the Way

In a far kingdom a greengrocer had three sons. The eldest son lacked courage. So the greengrocer sent him out to find someone who could give him courage. The son was given some money and told not to return home until three years had passed in his quest to find a proper teacher of courage.

The second son lacked persistence. The greengrocer set him the task of working in the store as an apprentice for three years in order to save enough money to pay for psychological treatment that would make him more persistent.

The third son lacked purpose. So his father ordered him to study for three years in order to discover a worthy purpose.

At the end of three years the eldest son returned home. He returned with courage even though he hadn't encountered someone to give it to him. The second son had saved enough money for psychotherapy, but he no longer needed help developing persistence. The third son found a purpose within the three years, but the purpose wasn't written in a book. He became a scholar.

Morita noted that by the time some people had worked to save up enough money for private inpatient treatment, they no longer needed it. The diligent, purposeful working itself had worked the "cure." So often it is in the doing and not in the being-done-to that we change in most important ways.

Chains

Samuel shuffled around the village with shackles about his ankles. From morning until evening you could tell where he was making firewood deliveries by the clanking sounds of the chains he wore. In his leather coat and apron, his hair neatly cropped, with a load of branches on his back, and those ever-present chains restricting his gait, he was quite a sight to behold.

Surprisingly, the chains were polished and gleaming each morning as he left his house. Even more surprisingly, Samuel wore the shackles voluntarily. He was the one who put them on in the first place. His story isn't well known, but it goes like this:

Ten or twelve years ago, Samuel woke up and headed outside to stretch and discover the day. As he set foot across the doorstep, he stumbled over dirty, rusted shackles. How they came to be on Samuel's doorstep no one knew (the story of who put them there and why is for another time and place). Certainly, he had done nothing to deserve them. His first impulse was to ask around town to find the rightful owner. But, then, who would claim such rusty old impediments? It would be tantamount to admitting some past crime, for only criminals wore such "leg necklaces." No, no one would claim them. No one wanted them.

Samuel had the odd notion that the chains had been given specifically to him. But if they had been made for him, why did they appear so old and rusted? The locks were open. The cuffs fit his ankles perfectly. Without really considering all the implications of what he was about to do, Samuel slipped the locks through their fittings and snapped them shut. Then he shuffled around the living room getting the feel of the things. And for some odd reason he kept them on.

In the days that followed sores developed on his feet from the banging and chafing of the chains. There were days when he considered trying to work his legs free from the metal wraps, but he knew he could not. As weeks passed, his legs and feet toughened. He became accustomed to the limitation of movement.

He began to polish the chains.

It was about that time that several bright young men came to discuss the matter with Samuel. They told him they could rid him of his chains for a certain amount of money. It might take time, but wouldn't he prefer to walk unfettered? But Samuel decided to keep them on. They fit him.

As the months passed, he wore the shackles proudly, whether they were gleaming in the morning or dusty as they dragged home in the dust of the evening streets.

In that small village it became a sort of custom for young people to imitate Samuel by decorating themselves with little silver shackles about their ankles. The shackles became jewelry.

The shackles have grown thin in places now. They could easily he broken. Samuel's legs are thick and strong from carrying the extra weight each day. He hardly notices the metal burden. There is no need to break the chains. Someday, perhaps, they will fall off by themselves.

Life sometimes presents us with responsibilities and obligations that hamper our freedom. An elderly, bedridden parent, a disabled child, a mentally disordered spouse, a failing business, a chronic injustice--all these are examples of situations that can place unexpected shackles on our time and movement. Some people have grown strong through these circumstances. Some, like Samuel, have learned to make even their chains bright and shining.

Filling up the Valley

Many years ago there was a long rope bridge spanning a deep valley. No one knew how the bridge had been put in place or who had put it there. One night during a violent windstorm the bridge was torn apart and flung away. Only its distant, tattered ends remained in the morning.

From that day one villager began to haul rocks to the top of the cliff overlooking the valley. The climb was steep and his load was heavy, but day after day he pushed and lugged hundreds of pounds of rocks to the cliff top and pushed them over the edge. They tumbled down onto the valley floor. Some of them were caught by the river and carried farther downstream.

Many of the villagers scoffed at this man's futile efforts. "You will never make a new bridge that way," they laughed. "How can anyone fill up such a vast expanse? It would take hundreds of years and hundreds of men to even begin to show some results. Look! The river carries away most of your effort anyway." They shook their heads at his foolishness.

Certainly, the loss of the bridge caused them much inconvenience. They had to carry their trade goods down the side of the valley, across the river, and up the other side to get to the local market. Nevertheless, this fellow's work was sheer foolishness! It would never change the conditions appreciably.

Yet he toiled on, day after day, month after month, year after year. Some days as he looked down into the valley, it looked as though a small pile of rocks had begun to form. On other days he could see no results of his efforts at all. Yet he continued with his task.

If you asked him why he carried on with such a fruitless task, he might have mumbled something about his desire to do something about the broken bridge, about the added suffering caused the villagers by the difficult trip to market. It was hard to find words for the restlessness he would feel if he weren't doing something, however trivial, about the problem.

One day this unnamed man died as he pushed a heavy boulder up the mountainside. Looking down into the valley, one could see little effect of his years of labor. Still, his face looked peaceful in death. Where there might have been a grimace from the exertion of years of effort there was only a smile.

There are many similar stories in Zen literature. One such tale is that of a small bird who tries to put out a blazing forest fire with the water it can carry on its wings.

Many important and worthwhile life tasks show no apparent results. We must undertake them not because we can accomplish them in our lifetime but because they are worthy of our effort. Working to relieve human misery is one such task. The satisfaction is in the doing.

Soft and Easy

The mud people of Planet Three were just that--they were made of mud. Their planet circled a sun that was sometimes hot and near, sometimes cool and distant. Some days the sun would shine; some days the rain would pour.

Put simply, there were two kinds of mud people. Some of them would work long and hard even on hot days, when the sun's orbit swung it near the planet. They received ridicule for their long hours of toil on these days. It wasn't, after all, economically necessary to work so hard. Mud people need very little in the way of creature comforts. Those who stayed out in the sun to labor on such hot days found their bodies baked hard as stone. They lost a certain amount of social status by their tough, dark appearance.

The other category of mud people worked only on cloudy, cool days. Mostly, they worked when they felt like working. They were known for taking a lot of time getting ready to work after they arrived in the fields, and they started getting ready to go home well before dark. They were respected and paid handsomely by mud-folk society. Their moist softness was a sign of luxury, beauty, and prestige. They prospered.

Until the rainy season came.

Anyone who consistently takes the soft and easy course turns out soft and easy.

Wings

In a castle town in Europe there lived three brothers. From the time they were old enough to go to school, they were obsessed with the desire to fly. The hunting falcons glided so effortlessly, then darted at their prey with power and agility. The kites tugged toward freedom above the castle walls. How wonderful it would be to soar in unbounded space! In time, the brothers became adults.

Karl, the eldest, studied birds. He knew the structures of their wings and feathers intimately. He dreamed and dreamed of being a bird. But he never flew.

Kurt, the second son, studied himself. He learned in detail the physiological conditions that prevented him from flying. He turned inward and brooded about his limitations. He never flew.

Kevin, the youngest, studied methods--the methods of science, engineering, mechanical crafting, business economics. He built models and prototypes and, at last, a flying machine. He flew.

When Kevin asked his brothers to share the seats in his flying machine, they refused. A noisy, dangerous mechanical contraption could find no place in Karl's dreams. Kurt felt no confidence that the device could carry him with all his structural weakness.

Only Kevin flew. He raced the falcons and circled the kites. Then he went on to invent other marvelous devices.

There is nothing wrong with dreaming, unless we only dream. There is nothing wrong with introspection, unless that is all we do. It is important to learn methods for effective action. Whether the methods are psychological or political or artistic or mechanical, they provide us with tools for moving beyond mental wheelspinning.

Our Constructive Living method emphasizes practical learning for practical living. When we have mastered the appropriate methods and have fulfilled one dream, we can move on to tackling the next.

Thirsty, Swimming in the Lake

In a country doctor's office on a Tuesday morning I overheard the following conversation. It was a metered exchange, with long pauses near the end.

"Nobody ever really cared about me."

"Nice looking clothes you're wearing, Ed. Pick them out yourself?"

"No, my wife did that. But as I was saying, Doc--"

"How long did you go to school?"

"I wanted to drop out, but my mother made me--"

"What did you have for breakfast this morning, Ed?"

"Just coffee. And I fixed it myself. Margie hates getting up in the morning. If she loved me more than that damn down quilt--"

"You slept at home last night?"

"Of course. Why--"

"I'm glad you made it safely to the office this morning, Ed."

"Huh?"

"Thirsty, swimming in the lake."

"What?"

"I said, 'Thirsty swimming in the lake.'"

"Doc, are you trying to tell me I should be grateful for what I've got?"

"Not at all, Ed. But it's important to notice the lake."

"All right, all right. But I feel so insecure. You know, Doc, farming is such a gamble. We've got debts to worry about. And they say they're ruining the atmosphere and a drought is gonna hit us."

"We can't walk on water, Ed. Have to swim."

"Hmmm. Reckon you're right. Don't feel like swimming much sometimes."

"Yep, me either."

"Sometimes dog paddling is the best I can do to keep from drowning."

"Yep, me too, Ed."

"Well, okay. I see what you mean. Thanks, Doc. Appreciate the time..."

"Glad you came by, Ed. Same lake, after all."

Venus

Once upon an unreal and magical time a lovely young lady wished for an ageless, firm figure and an eternally calm mind. At last she was granted her wish by the gods.

You may find her in the rose garden alongside the other statues.

X. *CONSTRUCTIVE LIVING* EXERCISES

Exercises in Living--The Ball Game

In this chapter I suggest some exercises for developing skill at everyday life, or in other words, at playing ball on running water. These exercises are by no means trivial. They are extremely difficult when done correctly, when done with attention and with purpose. You may wonder at first why these exercises are assigned. Perhaps you will no longer wonder after you have become accomplished at them. Very few people are skillful at all of them. Very few of my students are skillful at any of them when they first come for training. My thanks to the Constructive Living instructors who suggested some of the assignments below.

The first set of assignments are relatively straightforward:
1. Get up in the morning and make your bed.
2. Prepare breakfast.
3. Talk with someone.
4. Take a walk.
5. Clean the streets in your neighborhood.
6. Scrub your bathroom.
7. Eat dinner.
8. Play a game.
9. Take a bath or shower.
10. Go to bed.

The assignments in this first set need not be carried out in any particular order. You need not master one before starting on another. There is no time limit involved, although I expect that progress can continue for months and years. Before beginning on the list, you might want to practice with the following assignment:

Write a list of things that need to be done. I recommend a simple list for a start. The list should be relatively short, basic, practicable, concrete, immediate, and easy to tell whether accomplished or not. No grand items like "put myself through college," "find the perfect woman for me and marry her," "retire in the South Pacific." The list should contain items like "write in my journal every day this week," "get up in time to eat a balanced breakfast," "mail the check for the mortgage payment," "make five phone calls today for job interviews," "do dishes immediately after dinner," "take the car in Tuesday for servicing," "read ten pages in a new book," "shave every morning this week," "write a thank-you letter to Aunt Carrie," and so forth. Include some fun things--fun things need doing, too. But what goes on the list should be determined by whether or not it needs to be done, and not merely on the basis of its pleasantness or disagreeableness.

Someone suggested that humans should do something unpleasant every day as a sort of means of self-development, a subjugation of the ego. I'm not at all interested in that sort of thing here. I am very much interested in getting done what needs to be done, whether it is pleasant or not. Can you see the difference between these approaches? The other approach is focused on the discomfort or drudgery of changing the oil in the crankcase or cleaning the toilets. Constructive Living is focused simply on getting that oil changed and the toilets cleaned. The doer hardly fits into the picture at all except as a means of getting those tasks accomplished.

What a strange notion, you might think. Am I not important enough to be the center of my world? Shouldn't the pleasantness or unpleasantness of a task to me be the most important consideration when I undertake even some small project? I seriously doubt that anyone ignores the personal gratification or torment involved in his or her actions. But the greatest payoff comes to the individual who simply notes with attention that this necessary task is going to be interesting (or painful or frightening or exhilarating or embarrassing or some combination of feelings) and gets on about accomplishing what needs to be done.

Exercises Amid the Waves

Notice that I never suggest that when you feel ready you should continue with an exercise. You may not feel like doing an exercise and still need to do it. On the other hand, it would be proper to advise that when you *judge* yourself ready you should continue with an exercise. *Judging* takes into consideration feelings, but also information about our tendencies to be lazy and timid, the benefits of the exercise, and our need to do it.

Practice silent action. Try to wash dishes as silently as possible. Cook a meal with minimal noise. Work on your car or your house with attention to decreasing the usual clamor.

Pause before a meal and list twenty of the people who made the meal possible. Eat the meal in silence. With each bite silently thank one of the people on the list until all twenty people have been considered and thanked. (Adapted from an exercise devised by Gregg Krech).

Interview a couple of people over 65 years old. Perhaps your own parents fit this description. Ask about the details of their lives. Of what are they most proud? What did they plan to do in their lives but never got around to doing? What are their hopes and plans for the future? What did you learn from them about yourself?

Take a homemade snack or sack lunch for someone you don't know well at the office or at school or in the neighborhood.

The next time you feel down in the dumps call someone and don't mention a word about your own misery. Find out how that person is doing. Find out if there is anything you can do for him or her. Thank the person for talking with you. Go on to what needs doing next.

Greet a mailman, a truck driver, a toll booth operator, a waitress, a crossing guard. Smile and compliment them on something specific.

Write your will. Consider not only what material objects you will leave behind, but also what non-material traces will remain.

When you die what words do you want on your lips? Apart from the natural, "I don't want to die" or "Thank you" what final sentence would you leave with each of your loved ones? Perhaps you want to express those words to them now. What could you do today to live out your final words for them?

Exercises in the Rain

To be sure the best exercises are the natural ones emerging from everyday life. Our Constructive Living assignments are merely intermediary steps to mindful daily living. In a similar way, vacuuming can be used as distraction from immediate suffering. That purpose can be seen as an intermediary step toward the ultimate end of vacuuming just to get the room clean. Exercises provide novelty and learning opportunities at an accelerated pace. While undergoing Constructive Living training the assigned exercises actually became a part of "ordinary everyday living." All the while, reality sends you natural lessons before and after and even while doing the assigned exercises. Please be alert to learn from them.

No one knows what means are expedient or effective for teaching Constructive Living to a particular student. Frankly, we can't predict well at all which teaching devices will produce results for our students. What tale, what assignment, what maxim, what concept will nudge or boot someone into a moment of genuine understanding of this practice? So we set out the information cafeteria style, hoping you will select what you need from the servings before you. Here are some experiential exercises from the Constructive Living cafeteria.

Give yourself away

Patricia Ryan Madson, a faculty member of Stanford University, suggests to her Constructive Living students that they give away something every day. A number of other Constructive Living instructors also work on clearing away the material overload which plagues their lives by offering to others items which still have a useful life.

A dating game

Patricia Ryan Madson also recommends to her students who seek to socialize more that they invite others to go with them to do ordinary chores such as shopping, laundry, washing the car, and so forth. Such expeditions must be done anyway and don't carry the formality of a date. People deserve to be invited whether they accept the invitation or not.

Group rewards

Gregg Krech, another Constructive Living instructor, works not only on rewarding individuals for good performance but on rewarding an entire work group for achieving some stated goal through cooperative effort.

Credit where it is due

Gregg Krech also suggests selecting your finest accomplishment in life for reflection and discovering the specific contributions of others which allowed you to accomplish that feat. Similarly he recommends that you consider the specific support of others when you were at your lowest point in life.

Admiration where it is due

Another of Gregg Krech's exercises is to write the name of the person you admire most. Then write what you admire most about that person. You will find that under whatever you find admirable about that person is what he or she does, their behavior. What makes people admirable is what they do. We may make guesses about what they feel, but those guesses, too, are based on what we see them do. To become admirable people we must do admirable doings.

Setting goals

Professor Ishu Ishiyama at the University of British Columbia, offers this assignment to his students: Come up with a life goal then write down what you can do in the next five years to help achieve that goal. Then write down what you can do this year, this month, this week, today.

Encompass criticism

Make special effort to be accepting of criticism. Find the truth in criticism, the beautiful source beneath it. Don't allow yourself to be so distracted by the hurt you feel or the form the criticism takes to miss the positive information it contains. The Taoist approach to what appears at first to be a lie is to discover the truth underlying the words. For example, "I never make mistakes" may mean "I dread making mistakes" or "I find it hard to look at my imperfection." Take the same approach to criticism. Morita offered this advice about advice--thank the person who offers it, but you have no obligation to follow it. Do the same with criticism.

Charting daily activities

We may distance ourselves from reality with words. We may say to ourselves and to others that we have no time for some important projects. We may complain that we seem to accomplish little or nothing in our everyday lives. We may hold that life is boring, that we are lazy, that there is too much to do or not enough to do.

This daily charting exercise allows you to check on the reality of your everyday activities. It offers an objective record of what you are doing at fifteen-minute intervals during the day. A Japanese women's magazine with an associated nationwide organization, encourages its membership to chart such an inventory of daily activities. The members graph how they spend their time (and how much money is spent on what activities). It is an exercise well worth a try. You may find that you have substantial periods of time in between other activities, time which can be used more effectively.

The procedure is simple. Make a twenty-four hour chart with fifteen-minute intervals marked and space for writing a brief word or two about what you did during each interval. Words like "eating," "running," "sleeping," "watching television," "cooking," "reading," "lounging," "waxing car," and the like are sufficient. Keep an ongoing record during the day; don't try to recall the whole day's activities before bedtime. However, you may find it impractical to interrupt some activity to chart it.

When the activity ends catch up on the charting. Continue the daily charting for a week.

New Years Day activity

On New Years day try writing your epitaph, obituary, and eulogy as you might wish them to be if you were to die during the year. They should contain an account of your life accomplishments to date, and your plans for the coming year. It is a good way to remind yourself of the limited time within which you must do what needs doing. The same exercise might be repeated on your birthday and the results compared each year. The exercise is not about death itself, but about what you will accomplish before death.

Give a party

a. Make the theme a cleanup of the beach or a nearby park. Then provide refreshments and entertainment at the cleaned-up site.

b. Invite your friends to a quilting bee or some modern equivalent during which you make something to give away to the homeless, a nursing home, a mental institution, an orphanage. Check with people who have everyday contact with these institutions for an appropriate party purpose.

c. Throw a gardening party for a convalescing or new neighbor. Invite friends to weed the garden and shrubs and to mow the lawn. Then have a barbecue.

Going places

Pick an occasion such as your birthday or anniversary or holiday for this exercise. Write down where you expect to be and what you expect to be doing six months later and one year later. Write down some of the behavioral steps you must take to achieve those goals. Then put away these notes in a safe place with instructions to open them the same time next year. Check on how well you did. What goals were achieved? What steps went unaccomplished? Then write your expectations for the following year and repeat the process.

We do this exercise as a family project at my sister's home at Christmas. We open last year's folded sheets and read aloud our expectations. There is sometimes laughter as we compare what we expected with current reality.

Reminders

On a dozen notes write the question "What is my purpose now?" Post them in various places where you are apt to notice them during the day (e.g., on the phone, the calendar, a doorknob, a file cabinet, the refrigerator, the television) As you come across the notes consider whether you are doing what is necessary to accomplish your purpose. (Suggested by Daniel Hoppe)

Garbage thanks

Write a letter to the company which collects your trash praising its trash collectors for some specific service they have provided you such as taking the trash cans out of the enclosure when you forgot to set them by the curb. (Also suggested by Daniel Hoppe)

Scrambled Acts

Scramble the order in which you wash yourself in the shower, perform your morning toilet, eat breakfast, prepare for bed. The new order will require attention. (Also suggested by Daniel Hoppe)

Imperfection

Within ten minutes write down thirty of your accomplishments, great or small, from anything as simple as eating a sandwich to completing a college degree. Put a check by those things you did perfectly. Notice how many of your accomplishments have been achieved even though you did them imperfectly, even though you may consider yourself a perfectionist. (Suggested by Rose Anderson)

Reciprocity

Do a secret service (a service, however small, to someone without their knowing you did it for them) for the third (or fourth or fifth) person who does something for you after you put down this book. (Adapted from a suggestion by Gregg Krech)

Take a hike

It will take quite a few steps to work off the calories in a bite of pastry. Why not start walking even before you take a bite? Fred Paterno suggests moving your feet as though already on your walk *instead of* taking that bite. By the time he gets to about sixty paces Fred finds his enthusiasm for eating pastries has diminished.

Keeping track

A convenient way for keeping track of whether you got in your minimum ten thank you's every day is suggested by Gregg Krech. Put ten pebbles or coins in your left pocket and with each thank you transfer one to your right pocket.

Getting it together

Check out your understanding of Constructive Living by preparing a fifteen minute speech about Constructive Living to be presented to a specified audience of your choice. (Adapted from a suggestion by Barbara Sarah)

Comparative service

Offer two acts of service--one when feeling grateful to someone and the other when feeling no gratitude toward that person. How are the acts different? (Suggested by Barbara Sarah)

Clear separation

Repeat the following sentence several times: "David Reynolds (the name of a Constructive Living instructor or any advisor may be substituted here) is sometimes stupid, sometimes wrong." If you notice resistance to saying these words you misunderstand Constructive Living. If you say them with some glee, do more Constructive Living reflection. If you repeated the sentences in a matter-of-fact way with a sense of "of course" then it is likely that you have properly separated the Constructive Living lifeway (or advice) from the advisor.

No Small Matter

The trickle-down effect

Constructive Living trickles down into the smallest detail of daily life. Students are likely to find themselves turning off lights when not in use, using heaters less during the night, noticing the efforts of others that go into their daily bath. They notice that they are cleaning and polishing their shoes regularly, brushing their teeth more carefully, considering their pets' needs more, appreciating their food more, giving to others not because they have become different from them but because they see how much like them they are, becoming aware of the "aliveness" of food and machines and furniture and water and energy of all sorts.

In fact, only when it has begun to trickle down into the small crevices of daily thoughts and activities can Constructive Living really be said to have taken hold in one's life. Grand insight and deepened understanding are but momentary phenomena. Our existence is constructed on the bedrock of moment-by-moment living.

Rubbish

Attention to the detail of what we do helps sharpen our minds and refine our lives. I sometimes advise my students to make their trash beautiful. When you unwrap the paper from your hamburger what do you do with the paper? When you remove chopsticks from their paper wrapper do you wad up the wrapper and leave the unsightly thing on the table? How does your trash look sitting in front of your house or apartment building? How about the waste receptacles in your home?

Twenty years ago, as I first walked the residential areas of Tokyo, I was struck by the neatness of the trash set out for collection. Much of the garbage was wrapped neatly and tied with ribbons, looking more like something to be given as Christmas presents than like something to be abandoned. Even today, as Japanese finish their box lunches on the trains, they neatly tie up the empty boxes in the paper wrapping and deposit tidy bundles into the trash. Some Japanese fold the paper chopstick wrappers to make a functional stand to lay the chopsticks on when not using them. Almost everyone can fold the wrapper into a flattened form of half knot that is very presentable and decorative.

So what? Who cares? Trash is trash, isn't it? Once it is picked up and out of sight the problem of unsightliness disappears, doesn't it? Maybe not. If we take seriously an attitude of appreciation for concrete services from our world then wrappers and bags and rubber bands and staples and the like deserve some appreciation, as well. What is now trash was once our servant. It deserves respectful treatment. Sound strange? I wonder.

Rubbish, too, merits our concerned attention.

Walking

To watch a Zen master or a Kabuki actor or a classical Japanese dancer walk is to watch a lesson about living. The step is purposeful; the feet are placed one before the other with attention; balance is maintained throughout the stride. Walking becomes more than merely getting from one place to another. This taken-for-granted means of locomotion becomes an exercise of attention and character development.

It takes no great skill to make some educated guesses about people by watching the way they walk. There are mincers and swaggerers and prancers and totterers. But the way one walks need not be merely an indication of one's character and physical condition, it can be a determiner of character and physical condition. Use your walk to develop purpose, confidence, awareness, and health. Attend to walking well.

Walking is more than getting from here to there.

Coffee

Coffee or tea or plain hot water are warming, soothing, stimulating. Preparing and serving a hot drink can be automatic or engrossing, sloppy or artistic, character-eroding or character-building.

More than once I've drawn attention to the Japanese tea ceremony. The ceremony is simply the preparation and serving and drinking of a bitter form of green tea. How mundane! Yet how exquisite! The tea ceremony is exquisite because the movements and attitudes have been refined over generations and over years of practice by skilled participants so that every movement is choreographed for simplicity and grace.

How do you prepare and pour your coffee? How do you measure out sugar and cream? How do you stir? How do you raise the cup to your lips? Have you considered the behaviors and attitudes with which you participate in the simple ceremony of coffee drinking? From the moment of deciding to drink, through heating the water and taking the cup from the cupboard, until the cup is washed and put away, there is much to fill attention. When carried out properly, drinking a cup of coffee is no small thing.

Et Cetera

There is no need to detail the important elements of making a bed, writing a letter, dusting, dictating a memo, washing one's hands, brushing one's teeth, carrying grocery bags from the garage to the house, hanging up clothes, and the like. Each activity carries its own importance. Each offers the opportunity to build character. We must be careful to engage in attentively putting away the groceries because they deserve being put away in that fashion. If we try to put away the groceries carefully with the sole purpose of improving ourselves we run the risk of losing sight of the more important reality, the reality that the groceries need to be put away. The focus needs to be on the groceries, not on ourselves.

The by-product, then, of this aesthetic and purposeful action is the creation of an aesthetic and purposeful self. Again, attention to these small tasks is no small matter.

X. Constructive Living Quotes from the Water Books

Playing Ball on Running Water. New York, Morrow, 1984.

No one can heal a mind. p. 13

Reality doesn't respond to my will or my wishes or my emotions...it is what I do that affects my world...You don't need to change how you feel about something to affect it. p. 16

Insight alone is, for many, a way of avoiding making the effortful, sometimes painful, changes in behavior that are necessary... p. 17

No one can guarantee a life of good feelings. No one can guarantee that our efforts will bring the results we hope for. p. 18

To hold one of us responsible for another's behavior is meaningless for the one and demeaning for the other. p. 20

Acting on reality gets us some response from reality. And it is that response that tells us about ourselves in the world. We learn our true capabilities, our true limitations, and, invariably, what needs to be done next. p. 36

The purposes...are quite clear...to teach students to accept feelings as they are, to know their purposes, and to do what needs to be done. p. 51

There is a myth in our culture that something magical occurs during an hour of psychotherapy. I call it the myth of the golden hour. p. 56

Reality doesn't bring us things to do according to some ideal schedule that we have planned in our minds. p. 62

Patience may be developed indirectly through the act of waiting again and again. p. 62

I mistrust anyone who offers constant happiness, endless success, instant confidence, or effortless self-growth. p. 64

We don't need to know everything about everything before putting our bodies in motion. p. 71

Talk, talk, talk. How often it is used to back away from reality. p. 73

Confidence comes after we have done our work and succeeded, not before. p. 137

Anguish becomes more bearable when we know that we are doing all that we can to relieve constructively the conditions that cause the anguish. p. 143

Feelings fade over time. p. 155

Morita said that maturity isn't succeeding all the time; maturity is continuing to try even when we are failing. pp. 161-162

Even in Summer the Ice Doesn't Melt. New York, Morrow, 1986.

When you read below that we all have multiple personalities, that therapy shouldn't aim at the reduction of anxiety and depression, that every unpleasant "symptom" comes from a positive desire, that feelings are directly uncontrollable, that no one knows why we behave as we do, that change can only come about "now," that what we attend to is all that we know in any given moment, and that grief totally disappears when we don't pay attention to it, remember that the words were chosen carefully. p. 5

Part of maturity is taking responsibility for what we do, no matter what we are feeling. p. 12

There is no way to control feelings with any certainty and consistency. p. 12

After viewing our impotence it becomes more reasonable to ask the situation what needs to be done rather than trying to impose our will on it. p. 13

The myth of the self-made person is bankrupt. p. 14

There seems to be no purpose in digging for anger that someone else believes must be hidden somewhere in my psyche. p. 19

The simplified explanations of life built upon uncaring fathers and overprotective mothers and expectable feelings may have some value because they make us believe that we have a handle on why we are the way we are. But they aren't true. p. 20

What is certain is that I am sometimes this, sometimes that. p. 22

I don't need to understand (feelings) fully or to solve or to dissolve them somehow in order to get on with my life. p. 23

Reality keeps bringing us fresh moments with which to work, to live our lives. pp. 32-33

We are what we do. p. 37

Even the most unpleasant feelings are the natural result of our wanting to live and to live fully. p. 41

Fortunately, we have the ability to create a new past by means of changing what we are doing now. p. 49

It is all too easy to sidestep responsibility for what we do by labeling our problem an illness, a medical problem. But it is sheer absurdity. p. 51

My recommendation for the anticipatory anxiety he felt about undertaking a life outside the hospital was to go ahead and be anxious. p. 66

Continued complaining simply makes us skillful complainers.
p. 74

This attitude is part of the treasuring of all things because all things are borrowed. There is nothing that is truly mine. p. 98

Water Bears No Scars. New York, Morrow, 1987.

Much of psychotherapy as practiced in the West today is little more than clever conversation. p. 20

The assignment to greet one's neighbors is built on the recognition that neurosis grows as much from social/moral errors as from wrong understandings and unpleasant feelings. p. 21

There is nothing wrong with using common sense and wisdom in the psychotherapy setting. p. 21

Unpleasant feelings and sensory experiences such as anxiety, fear, pain, and discomfort are disturbing but indispensable to our existence. p. 22

Every kind of hurt directs us to some positive self-developing action. p. 23

Feelings fade over time if left as they are. p. 23

Focusing on feelings may prolong them, particularly when the circumstances that stimulate them reoccur. p. 24

A feeling-based life is in danger of extreme ups and downs. A purpose-oriented life or a behavior-oriented life is more stable and, in the long run, more satisfying. p. 25

Neurosis is not a disease of the brain or nervous system...it can be unlearned. p. 26

What we cannot change we must live with as we go about accomplishing our purposes. p. 26

The wage earner who goes to work early, returns home late, thinks only about office matters...is, in a sense, suffering from a life-narrowing obsession much like that of the symptom-focused neurotic. p. 28

It is possible to rest by shifting from one kind of task to another. p. 31

Life is built on moment-by-moment doing. those moments are all we have. p. 37

There is something about getting into one's running clothes that prepares one for running. p. 39

There's no need to get yourself to do it. Just do it. p. 41

Living constructively right now is cure. p. 42

In those moments when we lose ourselves in constructive activity, our neurotic suffering is gone. p. 42

Neurotic thinking is filled with the symbolizing that interferes with our seeing what reality presents to us. p. 44

We are all afraid of extreme change, uncertainty, death, fate, and "getting well." We often choose the familiarity of boredom and suffering rather than the uncertainty of change. p. 45

What you are doing now isn't "preparing" you for self-improvement. It either is self-improvement or it is not. p. 46

Life doesn't present itself in episodes or scenes. It is a continuous flow... p. 51

We organize our pasts to give ourselves orderly and memorable histories...we create dramas and villains and elaborate plots. p. 52

Can you already see that life never presents us with "problems," only with events?...Can you already see that the changeableness that is you need not be bound by labels such as "neurotic" or "lazy" or "coldhearted" or "lonely" or "insecure"? p. 53

Easing life circumstances won't allow the client to develop the confidence that comes from overcoming those circumstances. p. 54

It isn't that I don't care about my students' pain. It is just that trying to erase it will only cause more pain in the long run. p. 54

The satisfaction of giving to someone else while one is suffering, without mentioning a word about one's own plight, deepens character. p. 54

Rather than trying to become someone who doesn't feel the pain, it is more realistic and finer to become one who doesn't let the hurt dictate what one does. p. 57

I recommend to Stephen that he thank his mind each time that message of dissatisfaction appears. His mind will continue to make him miserable until he changes his actions. p. 58

Anxiety is natural. Shyness is natural. Anticipatory worry is natural. p. 59

Helen tells me her parents don't properly love her. I ask her to look at the specific ways in which her failure to hold down a job, her shyness, and her reluctance to talk to her parents have caused trouble for them. p. 59

But those who diligently look at the troubles they cause others and the favors others are doing for them find the exercise of great value. p. 60

To work and succeed and play and love while pretending it will all last, while ignoring the fragile "momentariness" of it all, is to miss the chance for depth in all these activities. p. 67

There is nothing ennobling about suffering itself. But in striving while suffering we move beyond ourselves to become new creatures... p. 68

Much of my work consists of saying the same things over and over again in novel ways so as to hold the attention of my clients. p. 70

In the past when Paul was true to his feelings, he was only acting in concert with some of his feelings, the ones he chose to focus on, the negative ones. p. 72

Some of my students aren't hurting enough. They hurt just enough to feel mildly uncomfortable and not enough to use the hurt to push themselves to make basic changes in their lives. p. 75

There is no use trying to make death pleasant or life free of anxiety. p. 75

The measure of an effective course or a wise guide lies in the pressure it exerts on the student to put into practice a realistic lifeway. Beautiful philosophical talk only prepares the student for more philosophical talk. p. 77

Don't work in the hope of becoming cured. p. 78

Scrubbing a toilet need not produce joyful satisfaction. It is enough that the toilet gets clean. p. 79

There's no need to try to psyche ourselves into believing how terrific we are. The reality is that we're not terrific all the time. p. 79

Cure for neurosis lies not in subtracting symptoms but in adding character. p. 79

Purposeful action in the presence of fear is what we mean by "overcoming the fear." p. 83

In his day Morita, too, encountered what I call self-growth junkies. They are people who run from one trendy self-development process to another, sampling each, mastering none. p. 83

For the graduate of this lifeway, summer is hot and winter is cold. p. 84

Some people try to cling to a teacher or a philosophical system to save them from their misery. p. 85

Put simply, reality has provided us with plenty of information about the results of self-centered, neurotic behavior. Whether we noticed the results or not is one issue; whether we acted on our observations or not is another. p. 86

Neurotically sensitive persons may want to see some grand meaning in a task before undertaking it. p. 86

We keep bringing our bodies back to the task until we finish it. p. 87

Most of us know what needs to be done most of the time; too many of us have developed intellectualizing, fantasizing skills that distract us from what we know needs doing. p. 88

Our wishes and direct efforts by will to make any feeling go away only serves to intensify it. p. 89

Those who want success most have the greatest fear of failure. p. 90

A strong desire or need inevitably generates a corresponding anxiety about failure or loss in that area. p. 90

Those without great doubts and great suffering are unlikely to produce great contributions to mankind. p. 91

It is not only that trying to cure oneself doesn't lead to cure, but also that trying to cure oneself is neurosis at that very moment. p. 93

There is nothing we can do to make sorrow pleasant. p. 95

Inactivity breeds inactivity. p. 95

Neurotics counter their own thoughts and arguments, too, leaving themselves paralyzed by indecision. "I could do this, but then that might happen," "I'd like to try this, but then I'd be prevented from trying that"... p. 97

The pressure to complain prevents the neurotic person from being a sensitive listener. p. 98

There's no need to understand some complex theory. I see not a few clients who are tired of trying to make sense of what their former psychotherapist was doing. p. 98

Repentance and guilt are necessary and healthy, however unpleasant and disturbing they feel. p. 99

When past mistakes can't be corrected through reconstructive action (when a parent has died, for example), then we must work to repay those we live with today for our mistakes of yesterday. What else can we do? p. 99

Morita saw quitting work as a great tragedy for neurotically sensitive people. p. 101

The immature person builds a self-image based on the appearances of others. p. 103

Enlightenment is acting realistically. p. 103

Morita noted that by the time some people had worked to save up enough money for private inpatient treatment, they no longer needed it. p. 108

None of us relishes taking a clear, cool look at our own limitations and faults. But reality is persistent. It keeps reminding us through a variety of means in a variety of situations what needs our attention and effort to improve. p. 116

Many important and worthwhile life tasks show no apparent results. We must undertake them not because we can accomplish them in our lifetime but because they are worthy of our effort. p. 118

Anyone who consistently takes the soft and easy course turns out soft and easy. p. 136

Acceptance may not eliminate the self-doubts, but the self-doubts become acceptable, too. p. 147

Successful people, too, have moments of despair. p. 150

There is nothing wrong with dreaming, unless we only dream.
p. 152

Nevertheless, with all this complexity, we must act. p. 154

Thirsty Swimming in the Lake. New York, William Morrow, 1991

We are truly ourselves only when we act. We define who we are by what we do. The locus of control in our lives lies in our behavior.

Feelings are a natural part of reality and must be accepted without direct struggle.

When we have behaved ourselves into destructive habits we must behave ourselves out of them.

It is easier to ponder the meaning of life than to fold towels neatly over and over again.

If there is to be religion, it must be woven through everyday experience. If you are searching for God you must find that Being within your stream of awareness.

Our own misery and self-centeredness interfere with our ability to see our parents' and others' efforts in our behalf.

Potential isn't worth anything until it is properly developed through education, self-discipline and hard work.

There is a voice that prompts us to change to more difficult work when we have mastered a task, when we are doing our best at work that is less than the work of which we are capable.

Feelings are natural. This moment's feelings fit this moment's me-reality; they are a natural element in this now.

Obsession boils down reality to rigid bite-size chunks that is no longer reality.

Recognizing and understanding our tendencies doesn't excuse them. Insight and understanding, like potential, are cheap.

Suggestion reduces the student's ability to make his/her own judgements. Suggestion narrows the student's focus

There is not steady climb out of harmful habits. Temporary setbacks and unexpected challenges are common. Hello anxiety. You again? Come on along, but I'm busy now.

Pools of Lodging for the Moon. New York, Morrow, 1989.

Effort is success. p. 16

Neurotic suffering grows from self-centeredness. p. 22

We can trust proper action to produce proper character. p. 26

We are just another means of achieving Reality's purposes. p. 28

There are two ways to live a marriage--with gratitude or with grit. p.33

Critical people operate in a world of faults and dissatisfaction which includes their own self-image. p. 37 We can assure ourselves misery by believing that we got where we are solely by our own efforts. p. 38

Feel despair but take out the trash. p. 39

It's quite all right to be the fool who lives life well. p. 39

Constructive living is more than making a living; it's my life. p. 48

When carried out properly, drinking a cup of coffee is no small thing. p. 55

When life (Reality) isn't going as we hoped or expected there is distress but also something to be learned, something different that needs doing. p. 57

Failure or even anticipated potential failure is painful in direct proportion to our wishes to succeed. p. 58

There is nothing I have learned in the scientific psychological West or the mystical East which makes me enjoy hurting. p. 59

Pain gets my attention. It says, "Do something about me!" Rational, logical arguments don't seem to have much effect on pain. p. 59

As I paint, what needs doing keeps emerging from the paper. p. 61

Attention to our immediate tasks, an active and positive life-style, and the acceptance of inevitable change as a part of human existence are fundamental to our Constructive living teaching. p. 63

Even within the dyad, neurotic love demands that one get one's own share. p. 67

Seeing so much of this imaginative drama, some people begin to believe that they are dominated by the same powerful feelings portrayed by actors and actresses. It isn't so. p. 68

We cannot generate gratitude simply by telling ourselves to be grateful. p. 71

Some people are hurting so badly that they want to be like everyone else. They are mistaken in two ways. They think that others don't hurt, at least in the same ways and to the same extent that they do. And they think that they can become like everybody else. p. 79

It is as though therapists were trying to teach a college course to patients who never attended grammar school. p. 83

Somewhere along the way you have to sleep alone. p. 110

When a house if filled with rights, there is no room for gifts. p. 111

If you think that what you are about to clean today will only be dirty again tomorrow, you'll never get anything done. p. 114

It is time to give serious thought to what psychotherapy is about and what it ought to be about. p. 192

A Thousand Waves. New York, Morrow, 1990.

We never have direct control over our natural feelings, but sometimes we can affect our affect by our actions. p. 26

The more we allow feelings to govern our lives, the more they spread to govern even larger areas of life. pp. 26-27 You can't make good feelings last and last; you can't make bad feelings go away at will. p. 27

We are rather like the cursor markers on the computer screen of reality. p. 29

The world just never seems to send us green lights and lottery prizes and kind words when we want them. And we want them nearly all the time. p. 30

Starting with our parents, our attitude shifts from how little we have received from them and how much more they owe us to one of how much we have received from them and how important it is to start working on giving back something to them. I'm not suggesting that all parents are perfect and that they have done a perfect job in raising us. But I am asserting that there were some adults in our lives who fed and clothed us and nurtured us when we were small. They did it whether they were in the mood or not, over and over again, whether we felt appreciative or showed them gratitude or not; or we wouldn't have survived to be here today. p. 31

The most joyful people I have known have all been people who gave themselves away to others. The most miserable people I have known have all been concerned with looking out for themselves. p. 32

Despite commercials to the contrary, looking out for number one is a sure path to torment. p. 32

Nearly anyone can make a living by offering some miraculous freedom from human suffering, some endless joy, some direct control over emotions...But people with their eyes on reality are beginning to see the foolishness and emptiness of miracle cures for living. p. 38

I haven't met a person who is free of suffering. p. 39

Constructive living helps you to recognize yourself as you really are, accept the whole mixed bag of you, and get on about living. Constructive living is a way to become nothing special. p. 41
As Morita put it, "The view from the high mountain is worth the climb." p. 41

We discover life meaning by acting in life, by doing. In the doing we create purposes as we go along...Most often

Each new moment is a birth and each past moment is a death for...all of us. p. 56

Life always implies desires that exceed realistic limits. p. 63

Neurosis is being caught by this discrepancy between what is desired and what is possible. Neurosis involves a misdirection of attention toward this inherently insoluble problem of life. pp. 63-64

To be alive is to need, to succeed and to fail, to be sometimes anxious and sometimes confident, sometimes regretful and sometimes satisfied. Life is just fine like that. p. 64

The danger of mental crutches is that sometimes they work...Then we run the risk of becoming feeling-centered again. p. 69

It isn't that my efforts now will result in success tomorrow. My diligent efforts now are success. p. 71

All the talk about motivation and addictive personality and mental readiness and decision making and positive thinking are ephemeral wisps compared to the truth of reality. p. 72

There are lots of hangers in the closets of our pasts...no single event 0 experience determines who we are. p. 75

Western psychology has taught us little about the operation of the human mind. p. 78

Both the Morita therapy and Naikan elements of Constructive Living require us to view every act as having moral implications. p. 82

Talking about Constructive Living is rather like hearing sports figures interviewed. Their talk is nothing compared to their performance. p. 83

Entrenched psychiatry departments stick to psychoanalysis and behavior therapy like they stick to IBM computers. They may not be the best and they may not be the most cost effective, but they are a safe managerial choice. p. 86

It is time that psychotherapists stop pretending they know what they don't really know. p. 87

We have been taught to focus on the faults and limitations of our parents and other significant others in our lives...We can blame them for our hang-ups and deficiencies. How convenient for us. p. 101

You can tell something about people's level of Naikan by observing how many paper towels they use in a public restroom or whether they leave the water running as they brush their teeth or how often they say or write thank you to their mother and father or what they do first when they come home from work. pp. 101-102

Unfolded pajamas means lack of proper gratitude toward the pajamas. Unshined shoes, an unmade bed, unwashed dishes are examples of the same principle. p. 103

In sum, then, it seems important for me to get on with living even though my understanding is terribly imperfect, even though reality doesn't meet my standards of ideal perfection, even though I am a flawed creature unsuited for easy accomplishment of many of the tasks I have set for myself. p. 108

Reality, the only show in town. Now playing. p. 133

In life you have to break in your own shoes. Some people try to do that by running away. 149

Rainbow Rising from a Stream. Morrow, New York, 1992.

Constructive Living (CL) is about being realistic.

Doing what needs to be done is about the natural, proper, fitting response to what springs from one's environment... Do what needs doing means fitting one's actions to the situation or circumstance. p. 16

You have been taught that feelings are the most important thing in your life. It isn't so. At the root of many problems in our country is this feeling-focus... You have been taught that you can "work on" your unpleasant feelings. It can't be done. Not only is it impossible to "work on" your depressed or anxious feelings; moreover, you have no need to "work on" them. p. 16

We invite our students to "try it and see what happens." We point out the undeniable truth that "you can't hit your wife if you're not in the same room with her." "You have no chance of succeeding on a job interview if you don't show up for the interview." p. 18

Constructive Living helps us take a realistic view of our imperfection, our unrealistic expectations, our flawed world. And we get on with our lives. p. 18

It is that very effort to eliminate neurotic moments from the mind that has caused some people to fall into an excess of suffering. Do what is right (not in some narrow moral sense, but what is appropriate, fitting, suitable to the situation), and the mind will take care of itself. There is no need to make a decision or commitment, no need to be empowered, no need to organize oneself or pull oneself together. p. 25

It is all right to dwell on past mistakes, to give up hope, to think negatively--while doing mindfully what is right in front of one's nose what needs doing. p. 26

Achieving some understanding of how our minds work neither gets rid of old habits of thinking and feeling nor eliminates the life problems associated with them. p. 27

In more recent times some people believe that salvation lies in discovering past childhood sexual abuse and allowing rage to emerge and be expressed. Salvation doesn't come that cheaply or that simply or that suddenly. Salvation, if such there be, must find itself worked out over and over moment by moment in life's eternal present. p. 28

Uncovering hidden feelings is rather like discovering hidden evil spirits and exorcising them. They don't exist, but if you can convince someone that they do exist you can charge them to get rid of them. p. 28

Neurosis isn't cured. It is outgrown or endured like an elder sibling's clothes. p. 31

Every feeling is a new feeling, just as every moment is a fresh one, emerging from and into Reality. p. 33

No amount of skill will remove our emotional reactions to disturbing or exciting stimuli..Emotions provide information about our world; to diminish them would be like wearing blinders. p. 37

Feelings send us important messages about what needs to be done in our lives. Don't forget that they are NOT the ONLY messages; they should not be the only determinants of our behavior. So working to "fix" feelings, instead of working to notice them and understand their messages, is a mistake. p. 37

My basic objection to alcohol and other drugs is that they interfere with our perception of reality. p. 41

Our eyes don't make reality holy, our actions don't make reality holy, it simply is that way. How reassuring! Because sometimes we forget. p. 46

Where do the fresh moments we experience come from? Where do our thoughts come from? Where do the words we speak come from? Where does the rich variety of Reality come from? p. 46

I want to put the mystery and transcendence back into our perception of everyday reality where it belongs. We can only see reality as "ordinary" by ignoring its magnificence. And so I resist making Constructive Living into a form of therapy, like Morita therapy and Naikan therapy. I want these ideas to be natural, normal parts of everyday life--not set apart as special techniques applicable only to the neurotic. p. 46

Delight brings the fear of losing the delight; success brings worries about sustaining the success. Good health brings concerns about losing it. The neurotic side of us finds the dark shadows surrounding every patch of sunlight. p. 56

What I am contending is that the discomfort we feel sometimes spurs us to do important things in our lives, and, sometimes, there are more important things for us to do than fight against discomfort. p. 61

We label the events in our lives "tragedies," "successes," "nightmares," "triumphs," "challenges," "defeats," and so forth.

Reality doesn't mind, It just keeps on presenting us with information that deserves our attention and action. What we do about what Reality brings us is up to us. p. 63

We all learn to live in spite of our knowledge that we shall die someday. Whatever fate has in store for us, the anticipatory anxiety cannot be so disabling that we cannot live fully now. p. 65

I never met a mind that didn't judge. That's what minds do--they discriminate, evaluate. Everybody's mind does that. What makes some humans stand out from others is that they don't let their judging minds push their behavior around. p. 72

Getting caught up in an obsession with perfecting the mind is itself a sort of narrow-mindedness. p. 72

A life philosophy is the product of one's life, not the other way around. We don't choose a lifeway and then live by it. We grow a life philosophy over years of living one. p. 74

When feelings are considered to be merely markers of past parental mistakes or signs of current psychological diagnostic categories or indications of the working of the unconscious (or other mystical, untestable constructions) then the feelings themselves are primarily tokens of "more important" phenomena. p. 77

Creative thoughts, like any thoughts, come from nowhere or some "unknownwhere" and flash into my mind. p. 79

Creative ideas and grand dreams are fairly common; actualizing them is much less common. p. 80

The best way to meet others' needs is not to be their obedient slave. That is mere cowardice and laziness. p. 82

We all have scrapes on our knees. Scrapes, too, are nothing special. p. 85

I used to think that some people were born with common sense and some were born without it. Now I know that common sense is earned by many experiences and many failures. p. 85

Reality keeps telling us that we do and die alone, no matter how many people are nearby. p. 86

Pride in oneself is a pale cousin to the much more solid confidence in reality. p. 87

Giving yourself away out of habit or timidity is merely inefficient and exhausting. p. 88

It is fine to be a beginner, even a fool. We can't be proficient at everything, especially at first. Experience gives us a shot at competency. Daydreams don't. p. 90

My earnings are the result of a cooperative venture whether I choose to recognize it or not. p. 104

The reflection aspect of Constructive Living ties us into the surrounding world with particular intimacy and the desire for reciprocity. p. 109

Constructive Living is not merely another language; Constructive Living is your native language. p. 125

There is Reality's work only you can do. p. 126

Happy birthday, Mom. Without yours I wouldn't have one. Love, Your child. p. 126

I've had lots of troubles in my life and most of them never happened. --David Miles p. 126

THE END

REFERENCES

Akegarasu, Haya. (Translated by Saito, Gyoko and Sweany, Joan) *Shout of Buddha*. Chicago, Orchid Press, 1977.

Brandon, David. *Zen in the Art of Helping*. New York, Dell, 1976.

Fujita, Chihiro. *Morita Therapy*. New York, Tokyo: Igaku-shoin, 1986.

Hoffman, Yoel. *The Sound of the One Hand*. New York, Basic Books, 1975.

Huber, Jack. *Through an Eastern Window*. Boston, Houghton Mifflin, 1965.

Hyde, Lewis. *The Gift*. New York: Vintage, 1979.

Ishiyama, F. I. A case of severe test anxiety treated in Morita therapy: Acceptance and not fighting it. *Canadian Counsellor*, 17, 172-174, 1983.

Ishiyama, F. I. A Japanese perspective on client inaction: Removing attitudinal blocks through Morita therapy. *Journal of Counseling and Development*, 68, 566-570, 1990.

Ishiyama, F. I. Brief Morita therapy on social anxiety: A single case study of therapeutic changes. *Canadian Journal of Counselling*, 20, 56-65, 1986a.

Ishiyama, F. I. Current status of Morita therapy research. *International Bulletin of Morita Therapy*, 1, 58-83, 1988.

Ishiyama, F. I. Morita therapy: its basic features and cognitive intervention for anxiety treatment. *Psychotherapy*, 23, 375-381, 1986.

Ishiyama, F. I. Positive reinterpretation of fear of death: A Japanese (Morita) psychotherapy approach to anxiety treatment. *Psychotherapy*,23(4), 556-562, 1986.

Ishiyama, F. I. Shyness: Anxious social sensitivity and self-isolating tendency. *Adolescence*, 19, 903-911, 1984.

Ishiyama, F. I. Use of Morita Therapy in shyness counseling in the West: Promoting clients' self-acceptance and action taking. *Journal of Counseling and Development*,65, 547-551, 1987.

Iwai, H., and Reynolds, D. K. (1970). Morita therapy: The views from the West. *American Journal of Psychiatry*, 126(7), 1031-1036.

Jeffers, Susan. *Feel the Fear and Do It Anyway*. New York, Harcourt, 1987.

Johnstone, Keith. Impro: *Improvisation and the Theatre*. New York, Theatre Arts Books, 1979.

Kapleau, Philip. *The Three Pillars of Zen*. Tokyo, Weatherhill, 1965.

Kennett, Jiyu. *Selling Water by the River*. New York, Random House, 1972.

Kondo, Akihisa. Morita therapy: A Japanese therapy for neurosis. *American Journal of Psychoanalysis,* 13, 31-37, 1953.

Kora, Takehisa and Ohara, Kenshiro. Morita therapy. *Psychology Today*, 6(10), 63-68, 1973.

Kora, Takehisa. (1965). Morita therapy. *International Journal of Psychiatry*, 1(4), 611-640.

Kubose, Gyomay. *Zen Koans*. Chicago, Regnery, 1973.

Laing, R.D. *The Divided Self*. New York, Pantheon, 1969.

Leggett, Trevor. *Zen and the Ways*. Boulder, Shambhala, 1978.

Maezumi, Hakuyu and Glassman, Bernard. *On Zen Practice.* Los Angeles, Zen Center, 1976.

Madson, Patricia Ryan. *Improv Wisdom*. New York, Bell Tower, 2005

McGee, Richard K. Review. *Contemporary Psychology*, 31, 10, 750-751, 1986.

Merton, Thomas. *The Springs of Contemplation.* NY, Farrar, Straus & Giroux, 1992.

Mills, C.W. Situated actions and vocabularies of motive. *American Sociological Review*, 5, 904-915, 1940.

Mitchell, Stephen, ed. *Dropping Ashes on the Buddha: The Teaching of Zen Master Seung Sahn.* New York, Grove, 1976.

Miura, Isshu and Sasaki, Ruth Fuller. *The Zen Koan.* New York, Harcourt, Brace and World, 1965.

Morita, Masatake and Mizutani, Keiji. *Jikaku to Satori he no Michi.* Tokyo, Hakuyosha, 1959.

Morita, Masatake. *Seishin Ryoho Kogi* Tokyo, Hakuyosha, 1983.

Murase, T. (1974). Constructive Living reciprocity therapy. In Lebra, T. and Lebra W., eds. *Japanese Culture and Behavior.* Honolulu:University Press of Hawaii.

Ohara, K., and Reynolds, D. K. (1968). Changing methods in Morita psychotherapy. *International Journal of Social Psychiatry*, 14(4), 305-310.

Pettingale, Keith W. et al. Mental attitudes to cancer: an additional prognostic factor. *Lancet.* March 30, 1985.

Phillips, Lakin. *A Guide for Therapists and Patients to Short-Term Psychotherapy* Springfield, Illinois, Charles C. Thomas, 1985.

Reynolds, David K. and Yamamoto, J. East meets West: Moritist and Freudian psychotherapies. *Science and Psychoanalysis* 1, 187-193, 1972.

Reynolds, David K. and Yamamoto, Joe. Morita Psychotherapy in Japan. In Masserman, Jules, ed., *Current Psychiatric Therapies*, 13, 219227, 1973.

Reynolds, David K. *Morita Psychotherapy.* (English, Japanese, and Spanish editions) Berkeley, University of California Press, 1976.

Reynolds, David K. and Moacanin, Radmila. Eastern therapy: Western patient. *Japanese Journal of Psychotherapy Research,* 3, 305316, 1976.

Reynolds, David K. Morita Therapy in America. In Kora, T. and Ohara, K., eds. *Modern Morita Therapy.* Tokyo:Hakuyosha, 1977.

Reynolds, David K. Constructive Living reciprocity therapy: An experiential view. *International Journal of Social Psychiatry,* 23(4), 252264, 1977.

Reynolds, David K. and Kiefer, C.W. Cultural adaptability as an attribute of therapies: the case of Morita psychotherapy. *Culture, Medicine, and Psychiatry,* 1, 395412, 1977.

Reynolds, David K. Psychodynamic insight and Morita psychotherapy. *Japanese Journal of Psychotherapy Research,* 5(4), 5860, 1979.

Reynolds, David K. *The Quiet Therapies.* Honolulu, University Press of Hawaii, 1980.

Reynolds, David K. Morita Psychotherapy. In Corsini, R., ed. *Handbook of Innovative Psychotherapies*, pp. 489-501. New York, Wiley, 1981.

Reynolds, David K. Constructive Living reciprocity Psychotherapy. In Corsini, R., ed. *Handbook of Innovative Psychotherapies*, pp. 544-553. New York, Wiley, 1981.

Reynolds, David K. Psychocultural Perspectives on Death. In Ahmed, P., ed. *Living and Dying with Cancer*. New York: Elsevier, 1981.

Reynolds, David K. *Constructive Living reciprocity Psychotherapy*. Chicago, University of Chicago, 1983.

Reynolds, David K. *Constructive Living*. Honolulu, University of Hawaii Press, 1984.

Reynolds, David K. *Playing Ball on Running Water*. New York, William Morrow, 1984.

Reynolds, David K. *Even In Summer the Ice Doesn't Melt*. New York, William Morrow, 1986.

Reynolds, David K. Morita Therapy in America. In Ohara, K., ed. *Morita Therapy: Theory and Practice*. Tokyo:Kongen, 1987. (In Japanese)

Reynolds, David K. *Water Bears No Scars*. New York, William Morrow, 1987.

Reynolds, David K. Japanese Models of Psychotherapy. In Norbeck, E. and Lock, M., eds. *Health, Illness, and Medical Care in Japan*. Honolulu, University of Hawaii Press, 1987.

Reynolds, David K. *Pools of Lodging for the Moon*. New York, William Morrow, 1988.

Reynolds, David K. Morita therapy and reality centered living. *International Bulletin of Morita Therapy*, 1(1), 35, 1988.

Reynolds, David K. *Flowing Bridges, Quiet Waters*. Albany, SUNY Press, 1989.

Reynolds, David K. Meaningful life therapy. *Culture, Medicine and Psychiatry*, 13, 457-463, 1989.

Reynolds, David K. On Being Natural: Two Japanese Approaches to Healing. In Sheikh, A. A. and Sheikh, K. S., eds. *Eastern and Western Approaches to Healing*. New York:Wiley, 1989.

Reynolds, David K. *A Thousand Waves*. New York, William Morrow, 1990.

Reynolds, David K. *Thirsty, Swimming in the Lake*. New York, William Morrow, 1991.

Reynolds, David K. *Plunging Through the Clouds*. Albany, SUNY Press, 1992.

Reynolds, David K. *Rainbow Rising from a Stream*. New York, Morrow, 1992.

Reynolds, David K. *Reflections on the Tao te Ching*. New York, Morrow, 1993.

Reynolds, David K. *A Handbook for Constructive Living*. New York, Morrow, 1995.

Roberts, Jim. *Deliberate Love*. Fairway, Kansas, N.L. Euwer, 2004.

Shibayama, Zenkei. *A Flower Does Not Talk*. Tokyo, Tuttle, 1970.

Simonton, O. and Mathews-Simonton, S. *Getting Well Again*. Los Angeles, Tarcher, 1978.

Soseki, Natsume. *And Then*. (Translated by Field, Norma M.) New York, Putnam's Sons Perigree, 1978. Suzuki, Daisetz. *The*

Training of the Zen Buddhist Monk. New York, University
Books, 1965.
Suzuki, T., and Suzuki, R. (1977). Morita therapy. In
Wittkower, E. D., and Warnes, H.(EDS.) (1977) *Psychosomatic
Medicine.* New York: Harper and Row.
Suzuki, T., and Suzuki, R. (1981). The effectiveness of in-
patient Morita therapy. *Psychiatric Quarterly,* 53(3), 201-213.
Szasz, Thomas S. *The Myth of Mental Illness.* New York,
Harper & Row, 1974.
Takeuchi, K. (1965). On Constructive Living reciprocity.
Psychologia, 8, 2-8.
Thich Nhat Hanh. *Being Peace.* Berkeley, Parallax, 1987.
Trungpa, Chogyam. *Cutting Through Spiritual Materialism.*
Berkeley, Shambhala, 1973.
Wilber, Ken. *No Boundary.* Boulder, Shambala, 1981.
Wilhelm, Richard. *Tao Te Ching.* London, Arkana, 1985.
(German edition 1978).
Wilson, William, transl. *Hagakure.* New York, Kodansha
International, 1979.
Wood, Garth. *The Myth of Neurosis.* New York, Harper &
Row, 1983.

Contact Information

Dr. Reynolds

Constructive Living

P.O. Box 85

Coos Bay, Oregon 97420

Telephone: (541) 269-5591

Email: dkreynolds@juno.com

Websites in English:

http://boat.zero.ad.jp/~zbe85163/

www.constructiveliving.ca

www.constructiveliving.com

Made in the USA
Monee, IL
02 August 2021

74809136R00144